The Seven Gateways

"A woman on a mission! My team and I have personally witnessed first hand, Benson's integrity in her business and her personal life. She is a master at discerning the next step, audaciously finding and eliminating fear, and dedicating herself to her ultimate destination of aligning her thoughts, beliefs and actions with God and the immovable laws of the universe. Wylene Benson knows what she is talking about."

>LISA SASEVICH
>Queen of Sales Conversion
>& Author of The Invisible Close™

"Wylene is a rising star. Spend any time with her and you'll experience meaningful connection, breakthrough and a desire for growth."

>KRIS KOHN
>Bestselling Author

"I am so grateful for the message that Wylene is bringing to the world. Her sincere heart and desire to truly serve makes her the right person to share this message of purpose, hope, and integrity."

>CONNIE BENJAMIN
>Author of My Fire Within
>Host of My Fire Within Radio Show\

"Wylene has a fierce dedication to living a principled life. I have had the privilege of witnessing the birth of this book and Wylene doesn't just write about the Gateways, she lives them and shares her personal process daily on her Gratitude podcast! The Seven Gateways are a faith-filled roadmap to a life of abundance available to everyone!"

>LISA CHERNEY
>Queen of Clarity, www.GFR.Life
>Host, Get F***ing Real show

"Powerful!! Wylene exudes purpose!! She possesses an authentic passion and is driven to expose buried purpose in others. I have personally witnessed the expert power bestowed upon her to listen, hear and guide others through confusion to their divine purpose. To see tears of hope, clarity and gratitude fall down faces is peacefully refreshing. She is truly gifted and a one of a kind breakthrough coach! This book is a must read!"

          CARMEN DAVENPORT
          Speaker, author and founder of InvincibleYouCoaching.com

"This isn't just another book. It's one amazing woman's life's work. Wylene is a giver and this book is a gift from God whom she serves by example. You will be a better person for experiencing the words on these pages."

          DAVID T. FAGAN
          Award Winning Bestselling Author and Former CEO of Guerrilla Marketing

"I work with coaches and influencers who want to create transformation in the world and influence people every day. Wylene Benson is a true influencer and genuine leader. Wylene leads from a place of spiritual inspiration and light. Her gifts come from real life experiences and anyone who has an opportunity to work and learn from her should consider themselves extremely fortunate to work with such a powerhouse of light. She is truly next generation in everything she does."

          TRAVIS BRADY
          The Coach's Coach & Leadership Speaker, Creator of Be Inspired Coaching, Host of "The 100K Coach's Podcast"

"We have been so grateful to have the opportunity to work with Wylene. We have been blessed to have the opportunity to work with her on discovering our own mission, vision and purpose which helped us to clarify where we should focus our time and energy in our business so that we feel that we are working in flow and not handcuffed to our business."

>CRAIG & JENNY DUMNICH
>Co-founders of Craig and Jenny D. Total Immersion Retreats
>www.craigandjennyd.com

"Wylene's very heart-based approach to life and business is not only refreshing but inspiring. Her desire to help others is unparalleled. Knowing her and interacting with her is infectious. Her sweet, direct, genuine and inquisitive nature is to be admired."

>SHANNON HUGHES
>Host of The Movement Radio Show

"Wylene is a heart centered leader that has a unique capacity to create breakthroughs and transformation in people's lives. She is sincere and kind, and lives day to day with a deep desire to see how much value she can create as she serves others. She is a gift to all those who are looking for ways to stand in greater integrity within their life and business."

>GERALD ROGERS
>VP of the Universe

"I have read a lot of books in my life on the topic of personal growth, particularly spiritual growth and emotional healing. But there were gaps in everything I read. And some questions were just never answered. When I first read Wylene's book, I was expecting a well-written but somewhat predictable text. After all, I have read A LOT of books! What I found in Wylene's manuscript illuminated my soul. The Gateways and the laws inherent in them clarified so much for me. Those unanswered questions were answered. Why is it so hard to overcome a scarcity mindset? Why do some once-good things sometimes just disappear from my life? In those moments of breakthrough, what was the catalyst? If you've ever wondered about anything like this, you're in for a treat when you read The Seven Gateways!"

> LARA HELMLING
> Founder of the Bestselling Author Studio
> and Forest City Publications

THE SEVEN GATEWAYS

YOUR MAP TO INTEGRITY IN LIFE AND BUSINESS

Wylene Benson

Copyright © 2019 by Wylene Benson

All rights reserved. No part of this publication may be reproduced, distributed, or transmitted in any form or by any means, including photocopying, recording, or other electronic or mechanical methods, without the prior written permission of the publisher, except in the case of brief quotations embodied in critical reviews and certain other noncommercial uses permitted by copyright law. For permission requests, write to the publisher, addressed "Attention: Permissions Coordinator," at the address below.

Forest City Publications
P.O. Box 2127
Loves Park, IL 61111
www.forestcitypublications.com

Printed in the United States of America

First Edition

To Clint
In Gratitude and Love

The Seven Gateways

TABLE OF CONTENTS

Introduction..1
Milepost 0: Choosing to Begin...5
Milepost 1: Choosing to Believe..9
    Key #1: Aligning with Truth..14
    The First Gateway: Faith...17
    Key #2: Pacing Yourself..20
    Key #3: Giving Yourself Permission......................................50
    Key #4: Discerning Truth from Counterfeit..........................54
    The Second Gateway: Abundance..57
Milepost 2: Choosing to Love..81
    The Third Gateway: Charity..85
    The Fourth Gateway: Prosperity..117
Milepost 3: Choosing to be Led...137
    The Fifth Gateway: Obedience..141
    The Sixth Gateway: Humility..161
Milepost 4: Choosing to be Whole...173
    Immovable Momentum...175
    The Seventh Gateway: Equity..181
Epilogue..207
Endnotes...210

PREFACE

The Seven Gateways has been a three-and-a-half year project that began with inspiration to write a business book for Christ-centered entrepreneurs and has evolved to become a guide for finding fulfillment in life, while at the same time, walking a path of purpose, where wealth and Christ-centered living fit hand in hand.

I believe that God intended for us to live abundantly, and to be happy every day through all our experiences. The world that He created for us is evidence that perpetual wealth exists. Nature is the supreme example of how predictably and perfectly we can systemize our lives and our businesses to have and be infinitely enough.

ACKNOWLEDGEMENTS

I am extremely grateful, more than words can express, for the talented individuals who helped me to begin and stay committed to completing my first solo book project.

I must first express gratitude to those dedicated individuals who participate live on my Daily Gratitude Call Podcast. The mastermind aspect of this call has exponentially increased the speed of change for me and I am inspired by their stories of personal transformation.

I acknowledge my mentors past and present. There are too many to mention personally. Nevertheless, there are two, without whom this book would not exist. To David T. Fagan for encouraging me to write a book. You continue to be a valuable resource in my evolution to legendary influence. To Kris Krohn, my first paid mentor. Kris, you taught me to give myself permission to expect and receive miracles. Your breakthrough process has been critical in my journey of alignment. It was the basis for my Permission Process which is a vital piece of my own signature Daily Rituals. I am grateful to you for the gift of total immersion, working beside you for the past six and a half years and counting.

Thanks to Kaylee Larsen, Arnold Kunes, Tom Porter and Laura Evans who each handed me a $20 bill to reserve a copy of this book five minutes after I announced I was writing it. Your faith was the catalyst to begin. Kaylee also became my first editor and helped me organize my original chaotic thoughts into manageable chapters. To John Bingham for asking the hard questions you knew my readers would be asking. Thank you for patiently encouraging me to find the answers. To Zeus Macias and Michael Laberdee for believing in the power of my message and using your unique talents to orchestrate the means for professional promotion of The Seven Gateways in ebook, print and audio form.

To Michael Sheen for your strength of character and gentle

prompting that helped me pull myself together in a moment of fear and doubt. You gave me the courage to grab opportunity when the universe presented it. To Angie Fenimore for your genius suggestions that gave life to the text.

And a special thank you to Lara Helmling, my final editor who has worked closely with me to keep my story and my message pure while encouraging me to boldly speak what I knew needed to be said. I am so grateful for your suggestions that improved the impact of this powerful message.

I thank my Savior, Jesus Christ for His example of integrity, and for providing the means for me to change. I thank my Father above who has the answers to all my questions.

Lastly, I want to thank my family for being so supportive of this book project, and of my choice to step out on my own to launch my business as a Purpose and Alignment Coach. The past year has been one of lessons and strengthening experiences that tested my resolve. I am so grateful for my own daily walk with God, finding peace within myself, my purpose, and my role as wife and mother.

THANK YOU

As a thank you for purchasing this book, I would like to offer you a special gift. Please go to my website: https://wylenebenson.com/contact-wylene-benson/

Contact me and request your gift using that form and I will send you an ebook version of this book, along with a mini-course called The Practical Guide Through The Gateway of Faith.

The guide is designed to complement the book you're about to read, helping you put key principles into practice for a brighter, happier life today and tomorrow.

Blessings,

Wylene

The Seven Gateways

INTRODUCTION

The Seven Gateways is your personal treasure map to a life of fulfillment. It takes you on a journey like none other you've been on before. You'll experience it all - the fun of beginning, the boredom of plateaus, the elation of the peaks, and the shortcuts that help you move around the obstacles. Through this journey, you uncover the most fulfilling way for you to make a difference living your life of purpose with integrity.

This is an interactive work encouraging you to take a quantum leap from an uncomfortable comfort zone into the void of creation, being equipped with the confidence to navigate the Seven Gateways and 'become' the person who is prepared to step into the new life that is most aligned with your unique Calling, Purpose, and Mission.

You will learn how to find your focus and stay true to the end result while letting go of control of how to get there. When you follow the map faithfully, the Seven Gateways will take you to a destination of freedom that is defined by immovable standards you set.

The Seven Gateways is your map to the life you're meant to live. It is the answer to your challenges in health, wealth, self-love and relationships. When you choose this way of life, you experience the lasting change you need. Perhaps best of all, you are then able to be a guiding light to your family, friends and community. The ripple effects of your legacy touch all of humanity.

Preview of The Seven Gateways

The Gateway of Faith - Recognize that I am enough and that all that doesn't currently exist within my scope of purpose will be provided.

The Gateway of Abundance - Act only when moved by passion/compassion. Immediately receive payment simultaneously as I serve.

The Gateway of Charity - Invite others into a creation that is truly my own, and expect them to be fully committed and in charge of only their part.

The Gateway of Prosperity - Enjoy the results that come when Faith, Abundance and Charity are present.

The Gateway of Obedience - Act when moved by love for my own joy and fulfillment of purpose, as well as the benefit my actions can give mankind.

The Gateway of Humility - Recognize my vital importance in the big picture. Acknowledge the source of my success. Create in harmony with the help of opposition.

The Gateway of Equity - I recognize my greatness as I see it in others. I acknowledge that each person's journey to perfect alignment is individual and unique. I give my best every day and seek the infinite equity of Jesus Christ to make up the difference.

The Seven Gateways

The Seven Gateways

MILEPOST 0- CHOOSING TO BEGIN

Wide-eyed and fearful, I lay on the thin mattress, vaguely aware of the erratic beeping of the machine behind my head. I saw the curtain flutter as feet hurried past in both directions. The buzz of voices and the harsh lights were like any other emergency room. But there was one definable difference, I was the one inside the curtain awaiting a diagnosis.

I was distracted from my surroundings by a crushing vice-like pressure in the center of my chest. I began to squirm and twist in an unsuccessful attempt to get away from the pain. Unbelievably, the pain was intensifying. And all I could think was, "What is happening to me?"

I felt the burning in the upper left side of my body growing stronger just as the technician whipped back the curtain and rushed in with his plastic tote. Yes! Maybe the tote carried something that could give me some relief.

"Can you give me something for the pain?" I pleaded.

"We have to check for cardiac enzymes," he said. "If this is an actual heart attack, the levels will be elevated." He added sympathetically, "I'm sorry, we can't give you anything for pain until we know the extent of the damage."

Before I could even respond, the needle was shoved into my vein and blood hastily drawn. I watched as several vials of thick red liquid were labeled and stowed in his tote, as he scurried outside the curtain.

The pain in my chest was excruciating. It had my full attention. The groans that involuntarily emanated from my own throat, the uneven staccato of the heart monitor and the quiet reassurances from my husband were barely audible by comparison.

I tried to focus, but felt lost in pain and confusion. A heart attack? It wasn't possible. Yet, the pressure in my chest was undeniable.

Finally, the ER doctor entered, followed by a nurse who administered a very welcome pain medication.

"Takatsubo" was the diagnosis.

"Takat…what?" I asked.

"Takatsubo, or Broken Heart Syndrome," he answered.

"Broken Heart Syndrome?" I confirmed.

"Yes," he said. He showed me the echocardiogram results and explained that the bottom half of my heart had simply stopped beating.

Broken Heart Syndrome. So seemingly random and yet so perfectly precise. In the eight weeks of recovery that followed, I would learn that my heart had been sending me a message that day, a message I desperately needed to hear.

The Seven Gateways

The Seven Gateways

MILEPOST 1
CHOOSING TO BELIEVE

Fresh out of college, I accepted a position as an office manager. The moment I took ownership of my very first swivel office chair, I recognized serious flaws within the office. The fledgling company was using a loose accounting system that had it just asking for an audit and limiting its credibility. After investing several hours choreographing a solid system, I asked for a meeting with the owner of the company. After presenting my case, supported by a three-page typewritten document complete with charts in full color, I was sent out the door with his laughter ringing in my ears and the words: "She's only been here two weeks and she's already trying to change our system!"

As this was my first real career, I felt that I must be the one in the wrong, that only owners and officers are important enough to be allowed to improve the structure and orchestrate the outcome of a business. I filed away my suggestions and committed to just being a good employee.

Five years later, I left that position to raise a family and try my hand at entrepreneurship for the first time. I joined a solid direct sales company, selling a product I loved. I learned much in my 18-year experience, gaining more confidence in business and in myself as a smart business woman. However, even after reaching one of the top ranks in the company, something was still not quite right. I felt as if I had climbed the ladder, but it was not as satisfying as I had imagined. I realized the problem was that it wasn't my ladder, and it was leaning against someone else's building.

Even with this new awareness, I didn't take the risk to strike out on my own. I began looking for another company and I did find something I loved. It wasn't long before I was once again leading a team. I felt confident in the value I was providing for a successful doctor's office. I took the reins as if it were my own business. Within a few years, the office could hardly run without me. However, my extreme dedication to the office, wasn't in alignment with the job description, and eventually I outpaced the pay scale. I had painted myself into a corner. I couldn't go on putting in the hours I had created for myself. Yet, I knew if I were to quit, the office would have a hard time replacing me.

I didn't realize it at the time, but I was learning a valuable lesson. As you will soon learn in the pages that follow, the Gateway of Abundance demands that equal value be returned for value given. If not, the Universe is out of balance and the agreement cannot be maintained. I had created a debt that couldn't be repaid. I had given far beyond the value that could ever be repaid in the position I was hired for.

Logically, I knew I had value and worth but it was all attached to what I could do for the other person. My faith in my abilities was tied to anticipating another person's needs, receiving positive feedback and recognition. The paycheck was just a bonus. My faith, self-confidence and ultimately my worth were only as deep as the words of gratitude and the pats on the back I received. I had to keep over-delivering to continue being seen as a stellar employee. That is how I eventually out-gave to the level that the universe could not reciprocate. I derived my value from serving. But the motivation to serve came from the belief that if I gave enough, I would be noticed for my value. To be noticed for my value was a result I could not guarantee. Therefore, I had a need that could never truly be satisfied long term.

You can never do enough when you believe you have to receive your worth and value from outside of you. Every gold star on the forehead is temporary and eventually wears off. Because it is temporary and inauthentic, the need to feel fulfilled becomes a bottomless pit.

I had created a no-win situation for myself. The only way to reestablish balance, would have been for my employer to promote me to business partner, because that was the job I was doing. But that option was not even on the table. It is interesting that when a relationship debt is created, it isn't long before the relationship begins to deteriorate. The other person can never reciprocate, so the partnership must end.

On a whim, one afternoon on my day off, I drove by my old office, the one where I had gotten my start just after college. I stopped in to just say "Hey!" It felt like I was coming home. After 20 years, some of the same people were there, and I was welcomed in as if I had never left.

That first visit turned into weekly visits. And those weekly visits turned into my creating a spot for myself to come back and work part time. Part-time eventually turned into full time and I left my position at the doctor's office to leap back into a place where I now felt I could carry my earlier commitment through to ultimate success. There was room to grow, and that felt exciting. After just a couple of years, I was being considered for the position of CEO. I knew this was my future and that my family would finally have a secure retirement plan.

On an ordinary work day in 2010, I walked into the corporate conference room. I brought with me, as always, my endless flood of ideas and an exuberant readiness to mastermind the decisions that would shape the company that I envisioned myself leading one day. In cultivating the future leadership team, it was not unusual for the company CEO to privately mentor me. However, on this particular morning, both executive officers were waiting for me as I walked in at the appointed time. To have both officers there was a little unusual.

As I sat down, I was a little puzzled as the two men stood up.

And then I heard a statement that stunned me.

"We are letting you go." said the CEO.

And then there was silence. I saw them steel themselves for my reaction. Perhaps even a rehearsed response if I didn't go quietly. What was I supposed to say? What was I supposed to think?

A hot sensation of panic shot through my veins. In that deafening silent moment, I saw my secure retirement, my ideal career, my dreams of helping the team I had been connected to for over two decades, being whisked away in an instant.

I realized I was holding my breath. For a moment I was speechless, trying to wrap my head around what was happening, and the long-term effects it would have on my future. A few simple words had just changed the trajectory of my life. It reminded me of how fragile the outcome of our plans are.

I looked into the faces of these leaders. I had trusted them implicitly. I had completely aligned my professional goals with theirs. I saw that I had been desperately seeking something from them, or through them. But what? What was I seeking? I wasn't even sure. It crossed my mind that perhaps I should have taken the hint all those years ago, that I am not allowed to lead here.

Through the pain I began to feel in my heart and my gut, as the imminent finality of the decision weighed on me, I consciously turned to a forced optimism.

So many thoughts ran through my mind in those few seconds after the CEO uttered those words. I was confident in my ability to secure another position. However, it was close to the holiday season and most businesses would likely wait until January to fill openings. And there was the question of my worth. Could I create something as promising at another company? Being in my late 40's and starting over was daunting.

I shelved my fears and determinedly stated, "That's okay!" And as much to assure myself as to assure them I added, "I have a lot of good years left. I know I'm good at what I do. I am certain there is another company where I can build what I had been hoping to build here."

I saw the relief wash over them and my former leader said: "I'm so glad to see that you are taking this so well." They both assured me that a wonderful letter of recommendation and a severance package would be forthcoming.

Inside I was shattered.

Why had it happened? Just as I was being considered for CEO? I asked these questions of God. I trusted His wisdom in allowing this event to occur and moving me away from this company, but what did it mean? What should I do?

His simple answer, and yet the most complex answer I've ever been given, was that I was out of integrity with that opportunity. Some people call this "outgrowing" where you're at. That's an okay way to describe it. In these pages, however, you're going to understand integrity, as I learned in the days that followed my exit, on a deeper and much more meaningful level.

Whether I'm speaking to groups or individuals, I often hear this question: what exactly is integrity? We all seem to have an intuitive sense of what it is, but few can truly define it. And honestly, many of those definitions are lacking.

Integrity is the result of discovering the truth within each gateway and aligning yourself with it. Integrity is not a final destination, but a choice at the exit of each gateway. You will find four questions at the end of each section, inviting you to evaluate your understanding of the truth versus the counterfeit within each gateway.

The Seven Gateways to Integrity is a progression. Each gateway adds to the previous one. Thus, integrity is achieved by integrating the wisdom you attain from each gateway while learning to recognize and embrace the truth. So let's get started navigating these gateways together.

Key #1 - Aligning with Truth

You must align yourself with the authentic version of the principles within each gateway before you will be allowed to pass. To pass through the Gateway of Faith, you must rid yourself of counterfeit beliefs about yourself and your value. You must look inside and see that you are already enough. You cannot move on to the next gateway, the Gateway of Abundance, until you realize that you already have abundance within you in rich supply.

Each gateway exacts a toll, and the price is your integrity, pure alignment, authenticity. Each gateway is a truth detector. Only when you can let go of the counterfeit beliefs that have blinded you will you be allowed to enter, and then enjoy the rewards that exist on the other side within the next gateway.

You will see, as we walk the gateways together, how I was living on the counterfeit side of truth. There is positive and negative in everything. In a sense, there are equally opposing ideas in everything we experience - there is the counterfeit and there is the truth. Our challenge is to recognize the counterfeit that is disguised as truth. Then when we discover the counterfeit, we must choose to cast it aside and unveil the higher truth underneath.

The Seven Gateways

The Seven Gateways

THE FIRST GATEWAY- FAITH

The Counterfeit

It was an outer game. I felt faith that I would find what I needed to succeed 'out there.' I over-gave value hoping for equal value to be returned to me. I believed I was good enough to take advantage of whatever opportunity I could find 'out there.' I couldn't see that I was already full of value, because I was looking 'out there' instead of within. The counterfeit of faith in myself is that I am enough when I do well. I can't see abundance (the next gateway), feel it, have it or enjoy it until someone else notices me.

The Truth

I was already infinitely valuable. The truth of faith in myself is that I already had what it takes. Whatever I lacked would be provided from the wide abundance

The lie of the counterfeit is so close to the truth, it is hard to detect. Once you see the counterfeit, it is clear that it is only a hair's breadth off of the truth. It's the truth with a catch.

that awaited me on the other side of the Gateway of Faith. But first, to be admitted through the Gateway of Faith I had to see that I am enough right now. I was the only one who needed to notice and acknowledge me. The counterfeit was that I had faith in my abilities. The truth is that I can have faith in my intrinsic value alone.

My Assessment
How I Crossed from the Counterfeit to the Truth

I am a savvy, charismatic leader with a gift for creativity and producing consistent remarkable results. My advice and opinion have always been respected and sought out by the top minds within the organizations I have connected myself with. I am independent, a self-starter. I see the vision of the desired outcome and my genius is a key element in navigating the many decisions and action steps required to assure the successful completion of a goal.

It is an understatement that I am extremely dedicated and committed. I know I am capable. My unique combination of business savvy and passion for creating something worthwhile is unmatched. I believe in my heart that any business would be blessed to have me. My desire to serve and make a difference has me leaping from opportunity to opportunity, diving in each time with total FAITH that I am enough and that because I am enough, things will always work out each time I leap. I am experiencing ABUNDANCE in my mind, because I love every moment I am pouring my gifts into the current project. I receive a paycheck of the heart immediately when I give. So why does each attempt at creating something really big, end with me getting kicked off the team?

Constantly taking a leap of faith towards something 'out there,' seeking abundance 'out there.' Finding a Cause to support 'out there.' Never realizing that there was something greater inside of me. I never considered that I had a Purpose and Mission of my own that others could align with.

The counterfeit is that I only see one way to utilize my skills. I have to find some place 'out there' where I can serve and where it will be appreciated. I feel the only creations worth supporting are 'out there.' In my immaturity, there is no knowledge of the possibility that a creation of my own even exists, nor of my own intrinsic value being utilized for my own purposes. I am living a shadow life of Faith and Abundance, constantly trying to attach myself to someone else's dream.

I do not recognize that I actually have a path of my own. By stepping into someone else's creation, giving abundantly and having faith that I can make it better, I am in essence trying to take ownership of their path as mine. This introduces tension in two ways:

1. It is not my path or purpose. This is fine, if my contribution complements the person whose path I am supporting. But if I am acting as if I am the creator and owner, I am in competition for the lead position. Rather than trying to lead, in order for me to be authentic and appropriate, I can be a support, nothing more.
2. The amount and type of value I am giving is out of balance with what can be equally reciprocated. By giving as if I own the creation where I am not the owner, rather than creating abundance, I create debt that cannot, nor should it be repaid. The full value of the success of the creation rightfully belongs to the owner of the creation. In this twisted attempt at abundance, I will never receive equal value.

Key #2 - Pacing Yourself

Continue reading to learn how the work you do in the Gateway of Faith produces the result of the Gateway of Abundance. With each Milepost, you will find that the gateways are paired. The first gateway of the pair requires your dedicated work and focus to step into authenticity. For instance, your work to develop faith in yourself and your future is the prerequisite to understanding and receiving authentic abundance. This gateway is about action.

The second gateway asks you to receive the gifts of the first gateway. If you're like me, it's sometimes much harder to receive than to do something. To sit back and receive feels like the counterfeit to our busy-busy-busy culture, but nothing could be farther from the truth.

When you do the work of the first gateway within each milepost, setting aside the counterfeit beliefs, you produce the effect of the gateway that follows. You get to receive that effect! Each pair of gateways works hand in hand to produce authentic results where you will be empowered to create personal success that is truly self-sustained and infinite.

Entering the Gateway of Faith

"Now faith is the substance of things hoped for, the evidence of things not seen." Hebrews 11:1

What is Faith?

When most people hear the word faith, they instantly think of it in a spiritual context, and they are correct in that all things are spiritual before they are physical. However, faith goes beyond just the spiritual. Then when you add the word 'gateway' to faith, the definition and application expands. Having faith is one thing, taking action within that faith is an entirely different scenario.

Like so many people, I love the Indiana Jones movies. In *Indiana Jones and the Last Crusade*, Indy was committed to overcoming three life-threatening challenges in order to find and retrieve the Holy Grail, said to be the cup of Christ that held an elixir believed to have the power to save his mortally wounded father. When he arrived at the third task, he was required to take a leap of faith across a deep and deadly chasm, far too wide for any mortal to physically jump. I love how the expression on his face changes when he fully commits. It seems there is a certain peace and calm that overcomes him just before he closes his eyes and raises his foot to take that first deadly step. It is the peace that comes when we give our all, holding nothing back in full faith, nothing wavering. There is nothing to lose because we have given it all away.

As you consider a leap of faith that you have attempted in the past, did you feel that your leap was like this deep and deadly chasm? Isn't that how all leaps of faith feel? We are brought to the brink of what looks like certain destruction, we look around and see no path, but we are still compelled to move forward by an internal source. Motivated by fear or by love, it makes no difference. Faith is required when we are at the end of what we know. It is just beyond what we see with our finite minds with our physical eyes.

Indiana's decision was not to blindly and frivolously throw himself off into the abyss with the false belief that a higher power would somehow reach out and catch him. It was one small step, taken with anticipation that more information would be available at the perfect moment that he needed it.

Of course, we were all equally astonished to see that the bridge existed all the time. It had been expertly camouflaged as a deterrent to those unworthy of the Holy Grail. Only those disciplined few who had prepared themselves to drink from the cup of Christ could courageously take that step of faith.

Our own task is similar. Each step we take prepares us for what is next. If we try to subvert a lesson, disaster is imminent. Consider this: if I received a million dollars and I was not prepared beforehand to be a good steward of money, the results could be catastrophic! The money would slowly slip through my hands, seemingly without reason or cause. This exact circumstance has happened far too often with those who have won a lottery or received a large inheritance.

Every step of faith has its challenge, to prepare us to receive ultimately what we desire. This means that every seemingly negative event on our journey is not to test and try us to the point of breaking— it is a necessary experience to prepare us to live comfortably in the new life we have chosen to create for ourselves. Every challenge is a gift, something to be grateful for.

When we see our challenges as faith-strengthening experiences to give us wisdom and preparation, we begin to welcome each obstacle with open arms. We may even begin to seek them out in order to arrive at our destination even faster.

But before we talk about finding the courage to take a leap of faith and overcome challenges, even to seek them out, let us first ensure that we more fully understand the concept of faith.

People have thought and written about the principle of faith for many thousands of years. Why? Because it is fundamental to human motivation and action. It is needed to perpetuate the evolution of the human race.

Ancient biblical writings define faith as "the substance of things hoped for, the evidence of things not seen." In this regard, we could say that faith is a goal or the desire to achieve a specific result. The second part of the definition tells us that we should seek "evidence of things not seen." Is there evidence of things not seen? Of course.

When I bake cookies, I don't have physical proof (a baked cookie) that the stack of ingredients on my counter (that I wouldn't want to necessarily eat individually) will make a cookie. But I have faith, and I have experienced prior evidence before, that if I put all these ingredients together in specific quantities and in a certain way, then I will have a batch of cookies that we can all enjoy. At the beginning of the baking process, I can't see the end result but there is evidence of its existence—or its future existence. The evidence is that all the ingredients needed for cookies currently exist separately on my counter.

This is truly the case with any goal or intention as well. All of the pieces and resources we need to achieve our goals are around us. If we haven't reached our goal those pieces just haven't come together in the right quantities and the right space and time for success. But they will...if we have faith.

We can't see electricity, but we can harness it and witness its potent effects. Scientists tell us that there are many things that cannot be seen, so they conduct experiments to prove their existence. When great mathematicians and scientists created strategies and trajectories to predict the rotation and speed of the earth in relation to the moon's gravity and orbit, we were able to put men successfully on the moon and bring them home again.

Did these mathematicians and scientists have positive knowledge that all of their mathematical equations and theories were perfectly factual. No! But they did have faith and they trusted in past successes. Plus, I might even go so far to bet they invited in some intuition and prayer. Eventually, they were able to find hard evidence to support their goal of putting man on the moon—but only AFTER they took a leap of faith.

A human visualizes a concept or object, which is not yet apparent or manifested. There is evidence of its existence in individual materials that already exist, either separately as an unrecognizable group of ingredients (like with the cookies) or already whole but in someone else's stewardship (like a pre-owned vehicle sitting at an auto dealership).

Using previous, known experience of our own or others, we can predict the eventual physical manifestation of our vision. We can trust that it will show up for us at some point in the future. But until it is actually revealed, and can be seen in the material world, we can only exercise faith in its existence in our future physical reality.

Fear Precedes Faith

Fear was my first motivation to exercise faith. I feared what would happen if I stayed on the same trajectory my life was taking. Once I took the time to hold still for a moment and really take inventory of my life, it didn't take a mathematician to predict the outcome of the trajectory of my course.

If you have never done this, take a moment right now and just focus on a negative situation that you have been trying to change for who knows how long. If you maintain your current course with this situation, what would your outcome be? Is it where you want to go? If you continue on this path, will you end up where you want to be?

For me, as I envisioned my trajectory, it was mediocre at best. It wasn't at all what I wanted for my life. I pondered my options and the fear overtook me with the realization of what would happen if I failed to change my course.

Fear can be a powerful tool. Once recognized, fear can be used to propel us off of our present course, and into another. Why don't we just calmly calculate the perfect course and easily change without dread? Some people do just that. Wise people who have mastered themselves and the art of utilizing faith in their lives do it. But most of the population aren't at that point yet.

I now have enough evidence that even a twinge of fear is a hint that something needs to change. However, at the start of my journey, when I first took stock of where I was and what my future looked like if I did nothing, I was one of the majority who was afraid. I was afraid of the unknown and uncharted wilderness before me. But as I contemplated staying where I was, I was just a little more afraid of the known—the mediocre life I was living. So my fear of the known propelled me to seek a new path, to change my direction, to leap into the uncharted wilderness with faith that I would eventually better understand the options ahead of me.

Faith requires that we use our mind's eye, our imagination to envision what we desire. I desired something more, therefore, I needed to become something more than I currently was.

My first leap of faith was to believe that I was really capable and deserved a better life. That was only possible after being willing to obtain a better view of myself. Opening myself to this naked introspection was scary. But in my vulnerability, I not only saw my weaknesses, I also began to see my strengths. To see myself as I currently existed was painful when I began catching glimpses of what I knew I could be. I knew I was not adequate to the task nor was I, with my current view of myself, adequate to maintain my chosen goal if I ever actually was able to achieve it. Faith requires that we use our mind's eye, our imagination to envision who we can be, and to believe that we can and will become it. If I wanted to eventually step into the life I was creating in my imagination, I had to become like a person who would have that kind of life, if I hoped to hold onto it.

I began surrounding myself with the kind of people who had what I wanted. I didn't pretend to be like them, or try to emulate them. I studied them. I watched and listened for characteristics that resonated with my own thoughts and beliefs and I leveled those areas in myself up to the highest truth according to my understanding in the moment. I asked questions of them and I also turned to my master mentor God, for even higher wisdom. I am so grateful for the guidance I received, both from the Divine and from my fellow travelers.

Exercising faith can be often perceived as difficult. To envision something that does not yet exist, and to believe in it enough to bring it into existence through our own efforts alone requires discipline and tenacity. To envision and believe in the better, more confident and influential version of me was an enormous stretch to say the least. I focused on faith, believing that if I could imagine it, I was capable of it.

One morning, I received a vivid, clear vision of myself in the purest form. Soon after recovering from the heart attack, I began searching my soul for purpose and meaning in my life, I had developed the daily ritual of clearing my mind of limiting thoughts, and asking to be shown step by step the choices and actions required to live and serve in a way that was in alignment with my God and my highest potential. I was very conscious of the time and knew that I needed to get moving or I would be late for work. Yet, my soul was crying out for some evidence that I was moving in the right direction, to know if I was really capable of helping people in a way that would make a difference.

Sitting in my quiet space, I earnestly listened. My body vibrated with the intensity of my silent plea. My heart was open to any hint that my desire was worthy of acknowledgement by the powers of heaven and earth. I heard...nothing.

I stood, and strode toward the door. I took only one step. That is when the vision came. Unveiled before my eyes, a tall beacon of radiance, wisdom and captivating beauty. She was a being of majesty and influence. Strong and magnificent, warm and inviting. I was shaken to the core, literally brought to my knees. The realization of my innate power and potential was awe-inspiring.

I was overwhelmed with the realization of what it would take for me to eventually measure up to the purest form of myself. Simultaneously, I desired to become that person. Like a mirage in the desert, the vision gave me sustaining hope. It was the answer I needed to keep going.

At first, that glimpse of my true self was emotionally and even physically painful. I doubted and judged myself as I currently existed in my limited perception. I knew I was not adequate in comparison to the vision I had been allowed to see. I also knew, with my current view of myself, that I could never maintain a significant level of success beyond anything I had ever achieved—if I ever actually was able to achieve it.

I held onto a quote by Marianne Williamson that I had often heard:
> Our deepest fear is not that we are inadequate. Our deepest fear is that we are powerful beyond measure. It is our light, not our darkness that most frightens us.

We ask ourselves, who am I to be brilliant, gorgeous, talented, fabulous? Actually, who are you not to be? You are a child of God. Your playing small does not serve the world. There is nothing enlightened about shrinking so that other people won't feel insecure around you. We are all meant to shine, as children do. We were born to make manifest the glory of God that is within us. It's not just in some of us; it's in everyone. And as we let our own light shine, we unconsciously give other people permission to do the same. As we are liberated from our own fear, our presence automatically liberates others.

As I reflect on the quote above, I am suddenly reminded of where I came from. My early family culture did not allow me to stand out in any way. To have a desire to be pretty was dangerous. To succeed above the family's financial level or to act outside of social norms was considered prideful. To desire a better life was downright disrespectful. I had spent my early life lowering my expectations to be acceptable. So when I caught a glimpse of the amazing being that I was destined to become, it took my breath away. Oh, how far I had already come, just in making this realization!

In a moment of clarity, I saw her. I saw the real me that I intuitively knew resided deep inside, and I was shocked to behold her.

There was no pride or desire to improve that prompted the vision. It came to me unbidden simply as an answer to a plea for faith in what I believed I was. There was an immense feeling of lack within me but because I felt certain of the truth of the vision, I found the peace and calm to take the first leap of faith toward aligning with her.

The 'truth' of what I beheld in vision became tangible in my mind, or in other words, it became the evidence or substance of something not yet seen in the physical form. It was an incredible experience that become known to me as my Gateway of Faith and my first quantum leap towards the ultimate life of purpose and alignment I was seeking.

In that moment I knew that the person I would one day become was in there somewhere, and that it would require time, tremendous effort and faith on my part to allow her to lead me. I experienced a profound willingness to sacrifice my former mediocre life. I surrendered to the vision of my future self, and became moldable, open to whatever would be necessary for me to become that person every moment of every day, not just in my private moments or in a moment of divine connection.

Committing to The Gateway

Let's identify the concept of the first gateway. As I said earlier, a leap is not a flailing hurl through open space. Instead, it is a deliberate action that quickly moves us from one space to another.

Goethe said, "Leap and the net will appear." Yet common sense tells us that it would be foolish and pointless to just leap without any concept of what you are leaping toward or why you are leaping. Remember Indiana Jones? He was deliberate in his choice to step from the edge he could see, into the unknown. The moment his motivation was based in fear for his father's life, rather than fear of the unknown, he had the courage to take the first fateful step. Once you have decided that your comfort zone is not at all comfortable and it really is time to take a leap of faith outside and choose something different, then it's time to investigate what really motivates you and why you want it.

So many people are simply resigned to fate and luck for what they receive in life. They do not realize that each person actually has control over what is created based on the words they speak and the emotion they put into their thoughts and words. But that is the truth—you get to choose what you want and you can proactively create it through your thoughts, words, emotions, and actions!

If you are just starting to understand the concepts of consciously choosing your life, you can look across the chasm that seems to exist between where you are and where you want to be, and even though you have never been there, you can possibly see evidence that others have created something similar. If you are a veteran at creating your life, you may be leading the way. If this is you, you may look across the chasm and only see fog and mist. No one has ever gone where you are going.

Whether someone you know has done what you want to do, or you're one of the first, the rules to getting what you want are the same, and first you must define and visualize what you want. You get to use your imagination to conjure up your perfect outcome. It will look different for you than it looks for anyone else. So even if you are following in a mentor's footsteps, the end result of what you want is uniquely your vision.

To be successful in your Gateway of Faith, be as clear as possible with your end result. Use every sense to create a clear scene. Bring into focus the people who surround you in your future reality. Listen—what are they saying to you? Is there a round of applause? Are there words of affirmation? Look—what does the space where you are standing or sitting look like? Are you outdoors, indoors? Are you in an event center giving a life-changing speech? Is your family sitting around you with love and gratitude in their eyes? Taste—are you sipping hot chocolate on the deck of your new family cabin overlooking a lake and pines? Smell—can you smell the sea air as you stand on your new sailboat? Be as specific and detailed as possible.

When you have your vision clearly in place, the next question you will ask is, why? Why, is almost more important that what, because if you don't know why, the first sign of a challenge or struggle can easily sabotage your success. If it gets too hard, it becomes easier to retreat to the old comfort zone. Your why must be bigger than your fear of the obstacle.

A question I like to ask is, "Why is this important to me?" Be careful that your why is not just on the surface, shallow, or for someone else. A common why I hear is "I want to help people." That is much too vague. Keep asking that question, "Why is this important to me?" Why is it important that you help people? Maybe the answer is "Because I want them to be happy.". That is the wrong reason. This has to be a motivation that comes from inside you. Making others happy is motivation that is focused on something outside of you. Besides that, it is something you can't control, nor is it your responsibility to make someone else happy. Keep asking yourself the question. Why is it important to you that others be happy? Are you catching on? Why is it important to you? The deepest motivation to remain focused on anything has to come from within YOU! And the most powerful is connected to your life's purpose.

We will dive deeper into the 'what' and the 'why' as we go along. For sake of illustration, choose something you have been wanting to change and visualize it as clearly as you can, the way you wish it would be. That is your 'what.' Then find a 'why' by asking that question, "Why is that important to me?"

Once you feel you have a clear vision of your 'what' and a solid 'why,' add emotion to both. Put yourself in the vision and just let the natural emotion of having achieved this awesome feat take over! What is that emotion? Is it love? Gratitude? Joy? Overwhelming compassion? Feel that emotion at ten times, one hundred times the intensity that you ever have felt that emotion before. Emotion sets the creation in motion. Without emotion, you will only be wishing.

Now choose a sentence or phrase that states what you are seeing, feeling, and experiencing. Include the emotions you felt, the people, the newly developed character traits, the confidence you are feeling, whatever you experienced in your vision, and put all of that into a present tense sentence or two about what you want to create.

Here's an example: "I am so proud that my dream of owning my own home is finally a reality. My wife and kids are so grateful for my dedication and focus in providing a secure life for them. Owning my own home allows me to finally feel the confidence of following through with something I chose for myself!"

Did you notice that I also included the human need of helping people? But it was stated and felt from your own perspective and what needs it met for you. You get to feel proud. You get to experience the dedication and focus. You get to see the gratitude in their eyes and the security in their body language towards you. You get to experience finally following through.

A leap of faith is an extraordinary moment, to which each one of us, it seems, must come at some point in our lives. It is necessary to face the choice to leap, or remain in mediocrity.

We progress as far as we can at any

particular level of existence, and the human need for growth begins pricking at our comfort. We can continue to do the same things and be the same person that used to make us comfortable, make all of the decisions

Most people don't realize that the fear before the faith is just the emotion of beginning a new adventure!

and do all of the things that used to feel comfortable to us within that level. But all of a sudden, those same choices don't feel comfortable anymore. At that point, until we make the choice to take a leap of faith, it will no longer be enough.

Each time we are willing to grow and improve and move beyond each plateau, we experience a little fear of the unknown before the decision of faith that brings joy and gratitude. Each decisive moment carries with it a rush of adrenaline that might be interpreted as fear. Sadly, most people don't realize that the fear before the faith is just the emotion of beginning a new adventure!

Those who are courageous enough to move forward in faith, will soon learn that the Gateway of Faith is the rite of passage to the next six Gateways. As with any rite of passage, once you have done it, you can do it again. The more you use your map of The Seven Gateways, the more predictable your journey becomes. The more predictable the process, the more you embrace the fear as just a prelude to faith. And faith is the gateway to everything you ever dreamed of.

Why Some Never Get Beyond Fear

Why do some never get beyond the fear and use faith to help them change a negative situation? Why do some stay in dead-end jobs or continue habits that rob them of health and resources? Why do some remain in abusive relationships? Why do they make the choice to remain the same?

I believe that a leap of faith in any direction would take them on a different course. It has been said that we cannot solve our problems with the same thinking we used when we created them. If the place they are stuck is truly not encouraging growth and creative expression, just making a move in any direction could shake up their world enough to illuminate a different path.

My motivation to change was born of my fear of remaining on my current known course. Although I had a good life, my course was stagnant. I was deteriorating. My life was unfulfilling. I felt I would die if I didn't make a change for the better.

I was brought to a point of vulnerability, taking an accounting of where I was on my life's course and being open to let the more authentic version of me speak bluntly. It is when we are in this raw space that we are most teachable. It's unnerving, but necessary. It's unsettling, but enlightening. You will see the gap between the current version of you and the real you. You will see how far off course you have gotten and it may feel like an impossible task to get back on track. Trust that regardless of your past choices and your current state, you are capable of getting back into alignment. The way is clearly marked through The Seven Gateways—Your Map to Integrity in Life and Business.

Where Do Inspired Shortcuts Come From?

The question naturally arises: if we are getting inspired messages to step out in faith, someone must be sending those messages, right? The answer is personal to each individual. For me, God is my partner in life and in business. He is the source of my inspired shortcuts and the miracles in my life. Jesus Christ is my Savior and He makes up the difference between what I am capable of and what is required.

Let your own understanding of yourself and your place in the vast universe be your guide. To fully embrace the principles I will be sharing with you, it is imperative that you believe there is something more powerful and wise than you, a higher power that has knowledge beyond human limitations. For me, that higher power is God.

If I believed that I was all alone in the universe and that the only resources I could rely on were those I could create with my own two hands, I would feel hopeless indeed. My belief in a higher power serves me and I invite you to consider as you explore The

Seven Gateways—Your Map to Integrity in Life and Business, that wisdom beyond human capacity exists in your life as well.

Trust your Higher Power to help you understand more about who you currently are, relative to who you have been in the past and also relative to who you know you can become. My own understanding of God has changed quite a bit since I began asking for guidance and wisdom from a source other than my own brain.

Part of the Gateway of Faith is to trust that everything that is needed to attain the vision I create in my imagination, will be provided to me at exactly the perfect time. The other part of the Gateway of Faith is to trust that I really am amazing and that I can do it!

Even if I did the very best I knew how, I would still need outside sources to help me navigate my blind spots. It serves me to believe there is a power outside of myself that cares about my success. It is a belief that I recommend, if you want to receive more knowledge than you currently have, in the precise moment it is needed. We can read books and hire mentors, of course. And I personally always have a book and at least one mentor that is guiding me at any given time.

I also seek to be daily divinely tutored by a higher source. The wisdom I gather from this source is digested instantaneously because I receive it only after I have been prepared to receive it. God knows precisely what is needed in the moment and always the exact step that is necessary for the actions of today. He also knows what I will need three months from now, so receiving a seemingly random (according to my finite mind) inspired shortcut today is just as important as one that seems right on target.

I invite you to move, to step with faith into the void of creation with me. Trusting that you are enough and that all will be provided at exactly the right moment. It is easier than you think.

Faith Equals Trusting your Inspired Shortcuts

How do you know if you are living in faith? I asked myself that question recently and I realized unless I had a tangible measurement,

I really didn't know. The answer came as an inspired thought that felt true to me: "When I take action immediately on my inspired shortcuts, I trust my source of information and I am in the energy of FAITH."

My husband and I have considered moving to a new home. This is definitely a decision I want higher information about. I can't see my future, so I choose to listen to my intuition about whether this was a good idea, and if so, what might be my first step toward this becoming a reality.

The simple answer that came to me was to get a bid for the repairs that would be needed to our current home if we hoped to get a good price when we sold it. The message was simple and something I could take action on immediately. So that very day I picked up the phone and called a contractor.

I didn't have the money in hand to have the repairs made yet, but I knew I had to gather information, and formulate a plan—in other words, create a vision—before I could know the path I must follow to get where I wanted to be, which was into a new home. Perhaps I couldn't finish the repairs that very day, but that wasn't the instruction. The inspired next step was to get a bid. and calling a contractor for a bid cost nothing, I could afford to make a phone call and to ask his professional opinions and get a bid on his suggested repairs.

I also had to get my taxes completed and filed, and I realized I had been reluctant to set aside the necessary hours to get all those numbers lined up and tallied. Because I saw this as an obstacle that could potentially keep us from moving forward, I set aside the required hours that day to begin the process of filing my taxes, just after making the appointment with the contractor. Two small simple items.

Remember, I had faith that everything I needed to move into a new home would be provided to me at exactly the right time. With faith, I found that as soon as I set things into motion, answers and means appeared in perfect timing. People and events showed up and happened in the very moment I needed them.

When the contractor came to look at my house, and as I was

asking him about remodeling the outdated bathrooms, something we absolutely could not afford at that moment, his trained eye discovered some water damage under the linoleum. On closer inspection, he deduced that the leak was probably from a pipe inside the wall. He dispatched a plumber who arrived that evening. The plumber was able to pinpoint the leak, cut a small piece of drywall from the wall and repair it all in one visit.

As I look back, I recognize that had I not followed my inspiration immediately, that leak could have caused a tremendous amount of damage over time. As it was, a disaster cleanup company came out with a couple of big fans that ran for a few days, the drywall was patched and the entire bathroom re-painted, the linoleum replaced and, Viola! We had an updated bathroom, all for the price of a small deductible when we turned in the receipts to our insurance company.

Next, I saw the front door to our 36-year-old house as old and ugly. I felt it needed to be replaced with an updated version to provide better curb appeal. I was initially dismayed to see that a compatible door would cost thousands of dollars to replace. Then, I noticed how much the beautiful new ones resembled our worn-looking door. The more I considered the new ones, the more I realized that our existing door would be very close to the new design, with just a little repair and an inexpensive fresh coat of paint.

Obstacle after obstacle was overcome in this manner, and we soon found that our current house was ready for the "For Sale" sign as soon as we found the perfect new home. When the time came to make the final payment to our contractor, we received a small unexpected amount of money that allowed us to pay the balance that remained immediately upon completion. Incredible!

I had never experienced anything like this before. All those years it felt like life was unfair. It seemed that things never went our way. Those beliefs were reversed with a single decision. The decision was to take a giant leap of faith and follow the inspired next step I had received.

I have discovered the Gateway of Faith is really less of a leap and more like taking baby steps. And again— it was not a reckless leap. Instead, it was a simple, deliberate choice to follow one inspired thought—an easily achievable step to call a contractor to get a bid, which cost nothing.

And the rest of the story is that we ended up loving the remodel so much that we decided to stay in our home, at least for the time being. So not only did we save a bunch on our remodel, we kept the same mortgage payment and increased the value of our home to boot!

The end result does not always look exactly as you envision it prior to committing to your new goal. It is always better! Repairs for our remodel were made with little financial obligation from us, I cleared out some clutter that had accumulated in the garage and basement for 30 years. I was prepared to move, that was what I envisioned. The actual end result gave us the home of our dreams and we didn't have to move! All because I was willing to use faith to immediately take action on an inspired message received from my higher source of information.

You Are Enough

You will learn more about 'enough' in the Gateway of Abundance. However, there is a core principle you must choose to embrace in this first Gateway of Faith, that will empower you to begin receiving. The Gateway of Faith teaches that you are as gifted as you imagine. Faith is also trusting that you will be given precisely what you need at the perfect moment.

I learned through my own experience that everything I would require to finish my goal would be provided when it was needed. Another principle I learned is that the highest version of me shows up when there is a challenge that is beyond my current ability. The only way I got to meet that version of me was by requiring more faith of myself than I had in the past.

Every time you act immediately on one of those inspired shortcuts, you gain evidence for the belief that you have everything you need. And the better you get at obeying your inspiration, the faster those inspired messages come, quickening your pace. Your success creates a ripple effect. As you act in faith, you can be the inspiration others need to believe in themselves.

Shifting from Fear to Faith

*You will never feel fully ready to do
something you have never done before.*

Each time I have stepped up to a higher level of being, I have not felt worthy or ready to accept what will be required to maintain the new level. But I have discovered a trick that works for me and I want to share my secret with you. I allow the version of me that is fully committed to courageously take the first step. Then I trust that the person I currently am will eventually catch up. Essentially, it's like a quote I heard once: "I throw my heart over the fence and expect the rest of me to follow."

Ultimately, faith is dependent upon your ability to believe that deep down you already are that courageous person who moves forward confidently regardless of fear. Ultimately, faith is dependent upon you intuitively knowing that you will be given everything you need in order to finish victoriously. If you don't have evidence yet, start with a desire to believe and the evidence will begin showing up. You ARE great! You just have been collecting the wrong kind of evidence. You will find evidence for what you believe. So change your beliefs.

Mentors can help when you don't have the belief or skill to reach beyond your limitations. They are also very good at inspiring you to keep moving because they have done it. Mentors can support and teach, but eventually you have to listen to your highest self and your source of inspiration of the next best step for you, and trust it. It is your path after all.

You cannot copy someone else's uniqueness. You must invent it from within yourself. It has never been done like you will do it. That is why your personal inspiration is the most important tool you have. What you want is closer than you think.

Hold Faith as Long as Required

I have a friend who had an amazing experience about holding onto faith while we were recently in Costa Rica. We had gone on a river float trip and spotted numerous varieties of wildlife including crocodiles, monkeys, toucans, and snakes. We had consciously stated at the beginning of the river float trip that we were intending to see a crocodile. When we did, it was time to level up the goal. I remember my friend saying, "Okay, now we need to see a sloth."

As night fell and we pulled the raft out of the water for the evening, our guide pointed out a dark blob thirty feet above us in a nearby tree and declared it to be a sloth. Sure enough, there was a dark blob, so we were sort of satisfied that we had seen a sloth, but not really.

On the bus the next morning, my friend sat by me and asked, "So how long do you hold on to faith in something you want to manifest. Like, we kind of saw a sloth last night, but not really." It felt like she was really asking, "Did I do something wrong?"

Just as she was finishing her sentence, four or five people on the bus yelled, "SLOTH!!!" Sitting in a tree, at a busy 4-way stop intersection, just outside the bus window at eye level was a cute female sloth. The bus driver was kind enough to pull over and allow us to walk back and take photos.

So what is the answer to my friend's question? "How long do I hold onto faith in something before it manifests?" You hold on to faith until it manifests! And you remain open and ready for the order you put in to the universe, to manifest in the most perfect way possible.

The other two sloths we saw on the that trip were extremely high up in tall trees. Only a powerful zoom lens allowed people to see them clearly. The best way for my friend to see a sloth up close was next to a stop sign at a busy intersection. And the universe knew it.

In the case of my home remodel that I just shared, we wanted a new house and we got one. But it didn't look like we thought it would. I thought my answer was to move, when really it was to remodel and just create a new version of our current home. If I had been really stuck on the idea of moving, I wouldn't have seen the gift in my own home. We did walk through plenty of homes while we were remodeling and we were very disappointed at what was available in our price range. The message we carried away from that experience was not that we don't have enough money to have what we wanted. It was that we have something amazing already that can't be replaced for the price. It gave us tremendous gratitude for what we already held in our grasp.

Taking Inventory

It is good to get a clear picture of what we have been believing and expecting regarding our ability, self-worth, potential, etc. Most days we live pretty unconsciously. We get up and eat the same thing for breakfast, go to work at the same job, return home and do the same activities without conscious thought. If we break out of the rut for a moment and just see accurately what we have been portraying to those around us, we may be surprised at what we find. Putting faith in something takes deliberate focus. Taking inventory up front gives us a good idea of what changes we need to make to prepare ourselves to receive what we are asking for.

Another reason to get an accurate perception of who we are right now is so we can celebrate the person we are becoming as we notice ourselves changing and growing. It is sort of like taking a 'before' picture. Then, we can envision the person we want to be—the person we must become—if we hope to maintain a higher standard. Focusing with faith on that person, rather than unconsciously subsisting day to day, clouded by past mistakes and perceived limitations, is the only hope we have of actually experiencing life as a more purely authentic version of ourselves.

Small course corrections are inevitable and welcomed as our vision clears. But it even takes faith, and a huge dose of courage to dive deep into vulnerability to honestly evaluate exactly how we have been showing up.

One of my clients shared that she was quite unhappy during the early years of her marriage. She recalled that as she was growing up, she had developed a vision of what marriage would be like, including the nature of her relationship with her future husband, and how they would move together along their path. When the reality of her relationship with her husband failed to match her vision, she remained unhappy for several years. Rather than divorce or despair, she chose to ponder on her marriage and her expectations.

She came to the conclusion that perhaps her vision had not been a good one. In retrospect, she admitted that her mistaken vision was based more on fairy tales she had read and seen in children's storybooks, than on the reality of the world around her. When she came to that realization, she made a course correction, and eventually reported:

> When I was finally willing to let go of that fairytale romance I had clung to so tightly for all those years, and began to focus on what I actually had in my marriage, it occurred to me that what I had was better. I just couldn't see it until I first let go of those preconceived notions about what the ideal marriage should be. My vision was juvenile, and the relationship I sought was not a fulfilling adult relationship. When I finally let that go and entered into a real marriage with my husband, it became very fulfilling, and we are very happy together.

Sometimes fear itself can be the best facilitator of developing faith. It could be the fear of hitting rock bottom and believing you may not bounce back, or the fear of poverty, or the fear of a failing marriage. It could be looking at what you have and feeling the fear of never allowing yourself to have more, or not knowing how to change.

As we discussed earlier, we also tend to fear the unknown, which is why so many of us opt to remain in misery. So we fear the known—the state we are currently in, but we also fear the unknown—the space beyond our current reality. The fear of the known counters our desire to grow; the fear of the unknown is the means by which we grow.

If fear is attached to the unknown, then, instead of retreating to the counterfeit of the familiar known, I am asking you to find the courage to sit with your fear until it becomes known, something you can be comfortable with. Allow those feelings of doubt, scarcity, anxiety to just be with you, until the reason behind the fear becomes known. When you do that, you step back into the known.

Regardless of what we fear—the known or the unknown—fear can be the stair step to faith, because fear is really just an indicator that we are about to become something more that we currently are. Trusting in that grander person we are to become is the transition to faith.

The battle between fear of the known and fear of the unknown is a state of confusion and indecision that many would rather skirt around, jump over, or avoid in any way possible. There is a point, however, during our learning process, our self-realization process, where we can begin to embrace the next step as necessary and welcome—which is probably why I no longer associate a negative response to fear. Identifying an obstacle that is always marked by fear, becomes a familiar experience, perhaps like seeing an old friend who always encourages you to stand a little taller and be a little bolder.

If I choose to, I can identify the feeling of being uncomfortable or vulnerable, as a personal 'weakness' and feel upset about it, or I can embrace this feeling as my newest adventure, an adventure where I give myself permission to explore all possibilities without judgment of myself or the results of each of my choices.

I have the choice to identify these learning moments as golden opportunities to learn what I need to know so I am prepared for the next step on my journey. I've come to realize that if I fail to avail myself of the opportunity at the time a fear presents itself, I will continue living at a level that is beneath where I am capable of going. Therefore, I welcome every new opportunity to examine a past shortcoming and make a new choice that is more aligned with the vision I hold of the highest and best version of me.

Preparation is Key

Let's say financial success is something to which I aspire. I feel that one million dollars is the appropriate amount of money to define my financial success, but upon self-examination, I realize that I'm not really prepared to be a steward of one million dollars. I presently lack knowledge about what to do with that amount of money.

If I received one million dollars in that unprepared state, the money might be squandered. I might have no idea how to properly invest the money to reap the rewards of its interest. My choices concerning my money may or may not perpetuate my wealth. Perhaps the best and safest thing I could do is just stick it in savings, and not touch it. But that sounds a lot like not having a million dollars.

I have a relative who on three different occasions received a fairly large inheritance through deaths of loved ones. In every circumstance, sadly, this relative used the money on unwise investments and frivolous spending. To this day, although he is very thoughtful and would give you the shirt off his back if you needed it, he is living in a ramshackle house and has very little besides that shirt.

Without becoming a millionaire first, most people are not prepared to be a millionaire. Preparing to be a millionaire is not something that just happens. It is something you have to work towards; it is taking a handful of tiny precise actions that shape the character of a millionaire. If I am not properly prepared—meaning, if I haven't become a millionaire in my mind, making millionaire choices—then I probably won't be a millionaire very long.

We must prepare ourselves for each new level to which we aspire, in every aspect we aspire to…BEFORE we arrive.

So how can we prepare ourselves if we can't prepare unless we already have it? Let me show you how I prepared myself for financial freedom without being financially free.

Before I learned the language and energy of money and a host of other lessons, financial freedom wasn't on my radar. I just thought it must not be in the cards for me and that I was destined to struggle financially all of my life. Generations before me hadn't figured it out, so why should I be any different?

But it was something I wanted, so I began preparing myself to live financially free. I started by surrounding myself with those who did have it figured out. I studied and gathered knowledge related to having money. I also invested in learning about real estate and found that, with a little education and some experience, it proved to be a fairly safe investment for me. Even the stock market has its systems that are somewhat predictable when studied and guided by a mentor. I found that there are many investment opportunities which are aggressive enough, and at the same time stable enough to provide sufficient interest and passive income to support me and my family. All this knowledge was gained through my own study and connecting myself with mentors who had more wisdom than I had. Gaining more wisdom and diversity of experiences is key. The mentors I turned to first helped me focus on my mindset. Changing my mindset was the single most powerful decision I made. My mentors helped uncover my blind spots and subconscious programming, guiding me gently into a new world where abundance and prosperity are the norm.

This mindset shift taught me to welcome money as a friend rather than something to be feared; an easily accessible resource, rather than something that was simply not available to me.

Each time I felt discomfort about money, I used the tools that I will be teaching you here, to change my mindset. In doing so, doubt was replaced with understanding. Worry was replaced with anticipation. Fear was replaced with faith. I am now comfortable with any level of financial success because I know the process to prepare myself to receive it.

"A lot of people in our industry haven't had very diverse experiences. So they don't have enough dots to connect, and they end up with very linear solutions without a broad perspective on the problem. The broader one's understanding of the human experience, the better design we will have." -Steve Jobs

That is what this book is helping you uncover—your desired end result and how to prepare yourself to receive it. When you are prepared to receive, anything you want will come to you. You don't have to worry about losing what you receive either, because it is only when you have not prepared yourself that it is likely that you will not keep it.

Key Indicators

Discomfort is part of the process of receiving and a necessary part of preparation. Every time we feel that twinge of discomfort, we need to recognize what a beautiful gift it is. This discomfort is coming to us in the precise moment we are ready to learn something big.

That first giant step into the uncomfortable void of creation happens really before we are prepared. As we keep moving forward, we bridge the gap between the known and unknown with our willingness to explore our discomfort and our ignorance. Supported by our determination to replace the discomfort quickly with knowledge and understanding, we can continue preparing ourselves with boldness and confidence.

The faster we recognize what we lack, and the more eager we are to change our perspective about it, the more likely we are to avoid much of the pain that often accompanies self-discovery and wisdom through experience. The more we resist and try to push away the lesson, the more discomfort we will experience, or—even worse—we may never make it through the next gateway. If we never get through the next gateway, we will never be prepared to receive anything new.

The Beauty of Opposition

I feel a short discussion on a beautiful concept called opposition is appropriate here. Imagine two people holding a rope across a river and pulling against it with equal force; the rope remains taut. If one person drops the rope, it loses tension and hangs loose.

Now imagine there is someone who desperately needs to get from one side of the river to the other, using only a rope. Opposition and tension becomes extremely vital to success. Without opposition the traveler will not succeed. The opposition is the very thing that creates a setting for success!

It is the same way when we are the traveler, facing opposition as we navigate the Seven Gateways. The opposition is good; it gives us something predictable to hold onto and shapes us into the person we need to become to achieve our goal.

There is opposition in all things, it must be so. Negative and positive forces constantly push against each other to keep the earth in rotation and to allow me to push against a chair to stand up. Choosing to love the challenges and use the opposition to your advantage will create more ease in your journey. The counterfeit of opposition is seeing it as a solid force that is trying to stop us. The truth of opposition is seeing it as a solid predictable law we can trust and use to our advantage.

Taking this to the next level is even more powerful. When we invite opposition into our lives, even seek it, we grow, change, and develop at an increased rate. Since we are inviting change at a more rapid rate, opportunities for success are more numerous and more frequently achieved.

Making a physical change, in the body for example, seems like a very long process. In fact, the physical manifestation is a byproduct of choices we make daily. The physical byproduct is the result of changes we are capable of making instantaneously— mentally, emotionally, and spiritually. We can train our minds to see ourselves as thin, long before the physical body looks thin to others. As the mind, spirit, and heart are changed, the physical representation of those changes naturally becomes the result. We do not have to force physical change. Having physical money is a byproduct of mental, emotional and spiritual choices. A physical representation of a loving relationship is a byproduct of choices made mentally, emotionally and spiritually.

Everything we want can be ours, as a byproduct of our thoughts, emotions, and spiritual commitment to it. Make the mental, emotional, and spiritual choices that align with the physical manifestation you choose, and it will be yours. Thinking, feeling, and choosing to be thin, wealthy and connected are prerequisite to becoming a thin, wealthy, connected individual.

To reach whatever goal you have, go to work on the mental picture, the emotional investment, and the spiritual alignment needed to bring it into reality. Do this daily and the physical representation will be yours in only a matter of time. It does take time. The physical change truly does happen immediately—we don't see it that way only because the physical is extremely slow compared to the speed of change mentally, spiritually, and emotionally. When we can line up these three, the physical change is imminent.

The brilliantly perfect part of making a physical change, is that there is ample time to create the habits to keep the physical change once it manifests. Physical structure and the rate at which solid energy moves, is a slower process. We put the energy into the other three (emotional, mental and spiritual) and we become the thin person before the thin physical body ever manifests. The time it takes is such a tender mercy. Because we are continuously being prepared to keep what we have created by the time we see it. And yet so many only see value in the physically completed goal.

When it seems to be taking longer than you wanted for your physical goal to manifest, don't give up! Don't order a cheap imitation either. You have placed your order with the Universe and it is being physically built. Hold out until it arrives. rather than giving up just before it arrives and ordering something else.

Allow me to share an experience when I didn't wait, and instead reordered something after I had ordered the perfect item. Before he passed away, my dad was a master craftsman with wood. He was a great example of creating something on paper and in the imagination, and then eventually presenting it to you in the physical form. I grew up smelling sawdust and paint thinner on a daily basis—those smells still bring back connective memories of visiting my dad in his woodshop behind our Georgia home. He built beautiful cabinets and furniture from solid wood that will last through generations.

When I was in the market for a new desk, because of my respect for good, quality craftsmanship, I knew I wanted it well built. I had specific features I desired as well. In addition, the desk I envisioned was a large executive style design with a decorative back that would be seen from the entrance of my office as I walked in. The desk itself would have keyboard and file drawers on heavy duty runners.

I created a picture on my vision board with all these details spelled out and began my search online for such a piece. I went to several furniture stores as well, and nothing seemed to fit—at least not in my price range. In order to have a hardwood style desk with life-time hardware, I was looking at thousands of dollars, and I preferred not to spend that amount. If only my dad were still alive! I knew he could create it for half the cost.

After a couple months of searching, I finally settled on price over quality. I found a particle board with laminate desk online that was smaller than I preferred but within my price range. I ordered it and was awaiting its arrival.

A few days later after ordering, I was driving and, due to some construction, was rerouted down an unfamiliar street. A block or so down the road, I noticed a yard sale at a commercial building. I glanced over and saw a dark, hardwood desk and actually said aloud, "Keyboard drawer! Two file drawers! Hardwood!"

I turned left across traffic and drove up onto the lawn to get out of the way of an oncoming vehicle. I jumped out of my car with it still parked on the grass, and ran up to the desk, looking for someone in charge. I actually sat on the desk and yelled, "I am buying this desk!" I had no idea how much it was, but it was perfect so what else mattered?

Someone came over and told me the desk was only $90. YES!! An hour and a half later, the desk was sitting in my home's entry and I was clearing a space for it in my office. The desk I had ordered online was already enroute, but luckily I was able to cancel it with no fees.

I had ordered my desk when I set the parameters in the beginning. I learned the lesson that it's important to believe the perfect item exists somewhere and that it is on its way. When you put something on order, don't order something else. Just be patient and keep your eyes open. It is there and waiting for you. The Universe will connect you with it at the perfect time.

Every time we order something, and we keep the faith until it shows up, we gather evidence of our ability to manifest.

Prioritizing Your Challenges

Some people ask me how they can identify what challenge to work on first. I have found that the easiest way for most people is to merely take notice of the stumbling block that is showing up right now. Take them as they come, especially if it seems to happen a lot. If you can say, "Why does this keep happening to me?" then you've probably found a gold mine of challenges to get started.

Reoccurring stumbling blocks are the no-brainer method of identifying a starting place for moving in the right direction. I teach my clients to question everything that is not currently working for them. As we analyze why these particular things are so vexing to us, and really seek the truth of them, we often come to discover something within ourselves that needs attention.

Something else I've noticed, is that, for most people, those very obvious obstacles must be handled first— before the subtler steps can be identified and taken out. It can feel like there is a never-ending reservoir of roadblocks, limiting beliefs, and doubts along our journey. I promise you there is an end to them. When you reach that moment of bliss, that is where chaos ends and creation begins.

As with all of us, taking the first leap is much like sprinting into a thick, dark, unfamiliar forest. And for most of us, there is only one thing scarier than sprinting into a thick, dark unfamiliar forest—and that is NOT sprinting into a thick, dark, unfamiliar forest, when we know what we desperately want is just on the other side.

Unless we are properly motivated—often by fear of the known, like bad health, social rejection, poverty, failure to succeed in business, or whatever the challenge currently is—we may forever languish in inaction. Yet, when we finally become motivated enough to take the leap toward a more perfect vision, we begin to see that our way is lighted as we go. That headlong sprint becomes a comfortably paced cross country run and the darkness begins to give way to the light.

Our fear fades with the light and lessons learned. We start enjoying the scenery around us, feeling gratitude for the newness of the experience and for the beauty and freshness of the vegetation. As the formerly dark things become illuminated at precisely the right time in the process, we take time to express gratitude for the gift of intuition and feel in our hearts that we are on the correct path.

You do have the ability to easily and quickly learn from every limiting thought, every perceived failure, every moment of doubt. Choose courage and begin your journey. You will be shown everything in exactly the precise moment you are ready to receive it.

The question now is: how do you best open to the guidance of the Spirit, of God, that will show you these things you need to know?

There are two vital processes—one is practiced daily (GPS) and one is practiced when an obstacle is identified and slows progress (Permission).

Daily Process for Finding Your Inspired Shortcuts
Your Daily GPS

GPS is an acronym for Gratitude, Prayer and Scripture (3 key components of the daily ritual). Your Daily GPS is actually a 7-step process that helps you get centered, visualize your goal, ask for your most important next step (which I refer to as your 'shortcut'), identify any limiting beliefs that would stop you from taking the shortcut, give yourself permission to proceed, and then confirm it with God through holy writings. End your GPS practice with a prayer of gratitude for all the information you just received.

Steps for Your Daily GPS

Step 1: Engage in some form of physical activity.
Step 2: Connect with your Vision Board and repeat your positive affirmations.
Step 3: Ask, "what is the shortcut to this goal being real in my life

right now?".

Step 4: Ask, "what is the limiting belief that would stop me from taking the shortcut?". Do your Permission Process and grant yourself permission to proceed.

Step 5: With eyes closed, flip open your Bible or other holy scripture and energetically allow yourself to be led to the perfect word, phrase or verse.

Step 6: End with a prayer of Gratitude for all you have received.

Step 7: Take immediate action on your inspired shortcut.

For a free video that shows you step by step how to have your own powerful GPS experience every day, go to www.wylenebenson.com/contact and ask for "Daily GPS - The One Critical Habit to Success."

Steps of the Permission Process

1. Notice that you are feeling a low vibration emotion that is based in fear.
2. Ask, "what is the limiting belief this emotion is tied to?".
3. Examine the cost of having this limiting belief. How will it affect your ability to progress?
4. Choose to let go of the limiting belief and give yourself permission to proceed.
5. Choose 3 new powerful beliefs to replace the old limiting belief.
6. Take bold action based on the new empowering beliefs.

My Daily GPS is the method I use whenever I leap into a new space, leaving what is known, to create something new. It has become the one dependable tool that is so simple and yet so little used by those who have access to it. Of course, in the beginning it was awkward and uncomfortable as I rigidly resisted the process. The more I was able to interpret my emotions and the more I proactively sought the lessons that would prepare me, the more comfortable I became in the process, and the faster my way was lighted as I entered each new dark forest of discovery. I have learned to live by intuition and to trust it implicitly. For most, this is a process of letting go and is extremely fearful. It feels like being out of control or giving away control. Ironically, in letting go and even giving away our control, we can most easily determine our outcome.

Within each gateway there is a truth that, when embraced, helps you easily move from one gateway to the next. There is also the counterfeit that distorts our view of the gateway, and will sabotage all following gateways if we move forward with the counterfeit rather than the truth. These counterfeit views happen due to decisions we make about ourselves typically in early childhood. It is not extremely important for you to understand why or how this happens. I am sure you will agree, however, that an authority figure making an emotion-packed assessment of a child, can leave a powerful impression that is difficult to let go of. I have adapted a quick permission process for this one specific purpose, to give you permission to believe something different if that assessment is causing negative results.

KEY #3 - Giving Yourself Permission to Proceed

The Permission Process was developed to help when we are stopped by a strong decision from our past that feels impassable. These decisions can culminate as thoughts like, "I am not worthy of good things" or "I am not good enough to do that." The Permission Process literally grants us permission to pass these sentinels that have been assigned to keep us safely in our comfort zone. Try it anytime you feel an emotion or thought come up that would stop you from confidently taking action on your inspired shortcuts.

Pick a Destination

Before you leap outside your comfort zone into something new, you must be completely at peace with what you're leaping towards. Until this point, you have only been at peace with it NOT happening. You have only felt peace with staying the same. So for the remainder of our time together, I invite you to choose something to leap towards.

There are three qualifiers for this leap. Choose a destination that:
- is not easy.
- stirs your very soul.
- is not possible in your current circumstance or state of mind.

Once you've chosen your destination, ask yourself two questions. Ask, "What if I don't make it?" and "What if I were not allowed to even try?".

If the fear of remaining the same is great enough to provide the spark for your leap from your comfort zone, then you've chosen a worthwhile endeavor. If not, go back and do the exercise again choosing a new destination.

If you are having a hard time clarifying your purpose and what is truly fulfilling to you, go to *www.wylenebenson.com/purpose* for free and low cost resources to guide you.

The Universe is Waiting to Take Your Order

I have many examples of how to step into your leap of faith. But it comes down to a few simple steps. For me, I recognize something needs to change, then I speak my intention—either by stating it out loud or by writing it on my to-do list. After that, I ask what the best next step is. Once I receive a thought, I take action. That action puts the manifestation into motion, and very quickly my intention is brought into existence. This only happens when I express faith by speaking the intention. Faith is present when you take a leap, until then it is just an idea with fear attached to it.

Fear and faith cannot exist in the same space. Choose to exercise faith and trust that the pure self within will guide you where you need to go. Trust that the pure self has the confidence and courage to leap. When you show faith by taking action, the universe moves in your favor.

As mentioned earlier, there are two gateways to pass through before you reach the next milepost. After moving through the first gateway, there is a rest stop, because the first gateway is where the work happens and now you need to take in all that you have accomplished. Get ready to receive. The work you have done to pass through the Gateway of Faith is going to produce new perspective and new wisdom that helps you receive the gifts of the next gateway – abundance.

Are you ready?!

To be sure that you have learned what it takes to be in integrity with authentic faith, take the assessment below.

Your Rite of Passage through the Gateway of Faith
How Aligned Are You with Faith?

Evaluate yourself on a scale of 1-5 (5 is completely aligned):
1. I am willing to leave my comfort zone and enter the pace of creation, holding onto a goal that I believe aligns with my purpose and desired end result.
2. I ask my Higher Power for inspired shortcuts every day, and I trust I have access to all I need to follow the inspired shortcuts immediately.
3. I listen for fears, obstacles and limiting beliefs...clues to the next challenge priority for me to break through.
4. I find evidence and believe "I Am Enough." I commit to aligning with the highest and best version of me.

Have you come into integrity with faith? Great! Congratulations! You have done the work to find faith in yourself, faith that you will be given all that is required but don't currently have, and faith to leap without full clarity of what you may find when you land.

Now that you have let go of the counterfeit of faith and embraced the truth about you and what you are capable of, give yourself permission to step into the Gateway of Abundance.

If your results have shown that you still have work to do on this gateway, stop and go back to the beginning! If at any point on your journey, you get stuck in the counterfeit of a gateway, every gateway that follows will only show you the counterfeit. Take the time to understand and integrate what you are learning. Align with the authentic version of you according to your new understanding, and enjoy the freedom of living a life of integrity and authenticity. Whatever you do, though, don't try to press on without coming into full integrity with faith first. Remember to do your daily GPS process. It can take a few months even to align yourself with this new truth. Be patient with yourself and enjoy the process, knowing success is inevitable when you do the work!

If you remain stuck, consider doing the permission process. If you'd like guidance, please contact me anytime and I can lead you to your breakthrough.

Key #4 - Discerning the Difference Between Truth and Counterfeit

If we believe the counterfeit, but we want truth, we will always be desiring something that is out of alignment with what we believe.

A lack of integrity between our desires and our beliefs will never feel right. Sabotage is the result. If you get stuck in the counterfeit of any gateway, you will be misaligned from that point forward. You cannot build authenticity and truth out of counterfeit beliefs. You will only see the counterfeit of all the gateways beyond because each one builds upon the last.

Counterfeit builds upon counterfeit. Truth builds upon truth. Each gateway requires that you be in integrity with the truth before you can see the truth within the next gateway.

The Seven Gateways

THE SECOND GATEWAY- ABUNDANCE

The Counterfeit

The counterfeit of the Gateway of Faith is that we only have value sometimes. When this counterfeit is applied in the next gateway, the Gateway of Abundance, a new counterfeit belief is created: we only deserve abundance when some judge says we are giving enough value. The reasoning here is that the gateway of abundance demands that we receive an equal or greater reciprocal value for what we give. If our value is conditional, then we only deserve abundance when some external source dictates that we are worthy. There is a catch to our value, and therefore there is a catch to the abundance we can enjoy. This is the reason so many struggle with money if they do not have faith in their own value. They believe there is only so much abundance and it is held hostage until they deserve it.

The Truth

The truth of the Gateway of Faith is that you are innately valuable. Therefore, the authentic effect that is created from this knowledge is that the Gateway of Abundance is waiting for you to choose from all the resources and opportunities within it, no strings attached.

"And if children, then heirs; heirs of God, and joint-heirs with Christ; if so be that we suffer with him, that we may be also glorified together." -Romans 8:17

My Assessment

I know that Abundance exists and I know that I can offer value. However, I believe that to participate in the flow of abundance, I have to seek out someone who knows how to generate abundance and who is also willing to share it with me because they deemed me worthy to receive it. The only way I can have more abundance is by finding ways to continually WOW those I believe to be the creators of abundance. I can never be enough because in constantly giving more, I eventually cross the barrier into relationship debt.

Entering the Gateway of Abundance

The Gateway of Abundance is the understanding that all resources are available to us at all times. Everything we need for our vision of the perfect life has already been created. Our faith in our end result and in ourselves is what draws the perfect resources to us. While you may have heard of the law of attraction, one fact that is rarely understood is that it is an immovable law. It is a law that cannot be defied, changed or avoided, much like the laws of physics. This law, like all other natural laws, is available for us to leverage. Thus, we can get predictable results whenever we use our creative powers of focus and intention.

The Gateway of Faith and all the wisdom we gain from it is necessary before we step into the Gateway of Abundance. Otherwise we may be creating an abundance of what we don't want! Using your imagination and asking questions designed to help you discover the place you are leaping to, prepares you to play right in the middle of your own personal treasure box of resources that was put together specifically for your purpose.

The world is divided into two groups: those who live in scarcity and those who live in abundance. Most of us live in both worlds at times, especially as we are familiarizing ourselves with the abundance that exists and which parts belong to us. There are patterns, habits, and deep-rooted beliefs that follow scarcity and others that follow abundance—Which one do you fall into?

Scarcity says there is only so much of any item. When that quantity is accounted for and consumed, that is the end of it. There is not enough of what we need in the world. There is not enough land, not enough food, not enough water, not enough oil, not enough wealth, and not enough of anything else that we want or need. There is only so much wealth, and we must divide it up among all the people. Then, when it has been distributed, that is the end of the wealth. This way of thinking suggests that if I get a little more today, it takes away from what my neighbor has now and what my other neighbor can get tomorrow. This belief leads to the hypothesis that all things are static and finite. It sort of makes sense, doesn't it?

But, is this true? Let's find out...

I am a master pie maker. I have made thousands of pies and often serve pie at events and casual get-togethers. If I have an apple pie divided into eight slices, once I've served up all eight slices to my guests, it's gone. And if someone gets a bigger piece of the pie, someone else goes without or receives a smaller slice. True enough. But is it really?

Does this mean that there is no more pie and someone really has to have less? It does not. Because I can always make more pie. Each time I make pie, I have an abundance mindset. To me there is nothing more uncomfortable than running out of food when I have invited friends in for an evening of connection. My personal choice is that abundance and connection go hand in hand. So I make more pies.

I live in a space of abundance. Abundance says that there is always enough—and more—of whatever I want, need, or desire. When I bake pies, there always seems to be at least one pie leftover after all the guests have gone. Does this mean that I made too much and now this pie has to go to waste? No way!

I have been known to run over to a neighbor's home and share a whole pie or a couple of slices because I had enough apples to make two pies and I only needed one pie. So back to the earlier questions: if I use more, does my neighbor go without? Are you starting to see the bigger picture?

When all of the pies I made today are consumed, is that all the pie? No! Next week I will pull a couple quarts of blackberries out of the freezer from my harvest last summer and the process begins all over again. There is no end to pie as long as I am willing to make pie.

What about ingredients? Will I eventually run out of fruit, flour, or sugar? No! This is because next year, my apple or blackberry harvest is even bigger than the year before because my tree is larger and I have pruned back the correct blackberry canes to encourage new growth and a bountiful harvest. Farmers are still growing wheat and sugarcane, and my hometown grocery store continues to stock flour and sugar.

If I did happen to run out of flour and was unable to get to the store, I could use my creativity to create flour out of something I already have on hand, like oats. My experience has taught me that oats ground in the blender are a great flour substitute. I see no end of pie ingredients for the foreseeable future. Yet, I'll bet if you ask around, there are some people who are wringing their hands over the eventual end of pie ingredients. Those people live in scarcity, but I live in abundance. And in abundance there is always pie.

In fact, there is always enough of whatever it is I want or need. This is an abundant planet that has everything we need, and there is a universe full of possibilities and opportunities. If we could see how large the planet is, from the view of a space station for instance, with all of the oceans and lakes, we would understand that there is enough water. And there always will be! Remember in third grade when you learned about evaporation? In my resident state where it snows, my kids learned that water first falls as snow on the mountains, it melts and runs down through streams and rivers to the sea, only to be evaporated and deposited anew on the mountains.

Those who value a scarcity mindset might say, "But if we drink the water, or if we use the water to grow our plants, then it is consumed and we will run out!" Is that true? What happens to water that is absorbed into a body, or into a plant's root? Does it cease to exist? No! It is eventually evaporated into the air and deposited again on the mountains. And even in the desert state I live in, somehow we have always had enough. How about oxygen—is there enough? Humans and animals breathe it in, and exhale carbon dioxide. Is there now too little oxygen, and too much carbon dioxide? No! Because trees and plants absorb carbon dioxide and release oxygen!

God created the earth and all the systems in and around it using the physical laws that govern our world to perpetuate itself. Humans are the ones who decide that there is not enough or that we need more than is currently available or that we need more than another person. It is a scarcity mindset that creates imbalance. What we focus on grows. That is Law of Attraction 101. Focus on scarcity and you will find evidence that there is not enough. Focus on abundance and you will always find evidence that there is enough.

Does this mean that we have to be happy and content with what we have and never seek to have more? Absolutely not. Being content means I am grateful for what is currently within my sphere of stewardship, and being content means I am also certain that there is enough and more available as soon as I have prepared myself to receive it.

The path to sustainable abundance is all about leveling up to receive and experience more than we currently are in charge of. But not just to have more—the reason to level up is to become more and serve more until who we are and how we serve are in alignment with the highest and best version of ourselves.

When we become a better resource to ourselves and others, we are adding to the abundance of the earth. Therefore, the cycle of abundance must reciprocate with more abundance to keep our world in balance. If our reason for getting is solely for consuming, we are diminishing the abundance of resources and eventually the Universe must reciprocate with scarcity in some form.

Perhaps it will be a scarcity in friends, trust, love, or new opportunities. Balance must be restored; the cycle of abundance must be perpetuated.

Most believe that there is not enough

Wealth is something I have in my possession that I can exchange for something in another person's possession.

wealth. Why? Because they do not understand what wealth is.

This begs the question: Can I create more wealth? Of course I can.
Anyone can. ake the example of baking those pies. Do they offer value to others? They certainly do. So if I use my resources to provide an increased number of pies, do I increase my ability to exchange my pie wealth for another kind of wealth from others? Yes, I do. In fact, I have done that.

Two holiday seasons in a row I found myself unemployed. I used my skill of pie-making to earn money for my family's Christmas gifts. Pie-making was not what I went to college for and it was not the trade I had chosen for my employment, nor have I ever owned a bakery or focused solely on pies as a business prior to that time. Pies was a creative way to use the resources I had (a skill at pie-making) to exchange for a resource I needed (income while I was seeking my next opportunity). The key to wealth is to recognize that we have access to it and there are limitless creative ways to bring it within our stewardship. We must be willing to exchange value for value. Sometimes that doesn't mean cash, sometimes our talents are our cash.

If one person offers money to another in exchange for goods and services, what does the person who gave the goods and services do with the money? He offers it to another in exchange for her goods and services who offers that money to another person for his goods and services, and on and on. This tells us that there is enough. That the cycle of wealth is endless. Just as snow becomes water we drink, and water we drink, becomes clouds that produce snow, wealth is a perpetual cycle that is always available to us.

There is abundance. Our economy is not a pie that is divided into 7 billion slices, then it is gone. Our personal economy is as large or as small as we want it to be. We determine how large or small our slice of the pie is. We each get to be creative in figuring out what kind of pie we will make, utilizing the ingredients available to us, and putting forth the effort in making a mouth-watering pie that anyone would pay money for. Our 'pie' could be stimulating conversation, a beautiful song, a morning radio show, or some other form of value.

As a nation, we determine how large or how small the entire pie is and how many pies we make. It is not fixed; it is not static. It is variable, depending on our willingness to produce.

This is not meant as a lesson in economics or planetary biology. It is a lesson in abundance. There is enough. The planet, the universe, God, and each of us are provided with everything we need and everything we desire, as long as we're willing to do our part to invite it into our stewardship. This is abundance.

How to Move from Scarcity to Abundance

On the other hand, some people desire to be taken care of or simply have never learned how to attract abundance, so they don't have what they desire, or even what they need. When they live in this space of wanting to receive but not knowing how to do so, it is easy to enter a scarcity mindset.

There are other manifestations of a scarcity mindset that many people don't recognize at first. Wasting (gathering more than is needed), over-consuming (just in case there is not enough later), and scaling back (trying to reduce in order to increase) are all examples of scarcity.

This is especially prevalent in abundant environments. For example, humans have basic instincts and finding enough food to survive is one of those basic instincts. Most of us have plenty in our pantries already, plus food is readily available in other places. In an abundant environment, basic survival instincts can cause people to over-consume or select foods that do not even resemble nutritional staples that their bodies really need. Both of these choices lead to health and social problems (neither of which is a byproduct of living an authentic abundant lifestyle).

A lesson we learn from the Gateway of Abundance is that to live in abundance requires conscious choice. I used to keep way more food in my kitchen and storage room than I could ever consume in a couple of years. My thoughts and fears of scarcity cost me in spoiled food and limited space. Replacing those fears with trust in myself and trust in the earth has helped me feel much more at peace. It has even given me a sense of self-reliance that if disaster strikes and there is a limit to resources, I will be just fine.

I am not choosing to have little, so that I will have to be taken care of in the event of a disaster. I am developing skills that allow me to be creative in how I might serve in that situation to add value. I am developing a mindset of confidence, trust, and faith that all is well regardless of my circumstances. These skills can be invaluable in a crisis, whether that crisis is within my own family or a nationwide epidemic. I resonate with the idea of having a supply of necessities on-hand. And, my conscious choice to see abundance all around me, engages the powers of the Universe in my favor regardless of my situation.

I freely accept as gifts those things that serve me, and I bring them into my life. Those things that I receive that do not serve me (like carbon dioxide), I exhale literally and figuratively. I return them to the earth for other life-forms to use for their benefit. If I hold onto stuff that doesn't serve me and that I can't use, it is like a poison to me and I am denying another life-form from the very breath that sustains it. Even having three vacuum cleaners when I only need one could be depriving myself of abundant usable real estate in my home. It could also be that there is someone who has zero vacuum cleaners, and that would totally be feeling abundant because they were able to purchase a good vacuum cleaner at my yard sale.

One of the lessons of the Gateway of Abundance is that there are certain building materials that belong to me, and some that belong to others. The rite of passage through the Gateway of Abundance includes noticing what we are hoarding that belongs to someone else. When we can begin to see the needs of others with equal importance to our own, we are on our way through the Gateway of Abundance.

Being in tune with abundance helps us realize that there is no need to compete for it. The race to stock away more than others is unnecessary. There is enough. One way to put ourselves in a state of abundance is by repeating positive affirmations about abundance. Here is a mantra of abundance that I have formulated for my life: I give freely of my abundance, as the earth does, and I continue to maintain and recreate myself. I am abundant.

Have I always had an abundance mentality? In some ways I could say yes, because even as a child I enjoyed the feeling that I always had enough. However, as with all of the gateways in life, many concepts and principles seem to ebb and flow in our hearts, and we experience them with greater and lesser intensity at various times.

A perfect example of scarcity occurred in my life when I felt that I had to fix up my home to sell it and move to another. My scarcity mindset prevented me from seeing any other way to accomplish this goal of moving. In my mind, there was no getting around the idea that I had remodel our home and I had insufficient resources in my bank account to make it happen. When abundance returned to my heart, I found that I had everything within my grasp needed to prepare my home for sale and get it on the market, without my bank account even being touched. And in the end, for a small investment I created a brand new home for myself and I didn't even have to move!

The only thing that changed from one moment to the next was my mindset. In taking my leap of faith that day I called the contractor for a bid, I simultaneously entered the space where abundance exists. I trusted that all that was needful was already mine. I gathered together what I knew I had, and awaiting the next inspired step. Taking the first step made the next step instantly known to me. Combining a faith mindset with an abundance mindset, we always know what the next step is in the perfect moment, and all resources are available to complete it.

The key to moving from scarcity to abundance is gratitude. When we can be grateful and content for what is, we automatically begin to see all the things there are to be grateful for. We find evidence that there is enough.

Turning on the Flow of Abundance

The cycle of abundance begins with giving. In the same way the earth gives to us in great abundance, we can freely share what we have and create abundance for those around us. Additionally, in creating space by letting go of something (like giving away the extra vacuum cleaner), you make room for something new and even better to come back to you. Plus, you sharing with others, gives them evidence of abundance in their lives as well.

In the same way, by giving away your skill, time, talent, money, etc., you create extra space to receive something new—making you more abundant. You give something you have in abundance, in order to receive something that you desire. This is the cycle of abundance, and giving is at the beginning of it all.

Receiving the return on your gift of abundance doesn't always come immediately after giving, but I want to share one of several examples in my life when it absolutely did. A business associate came to my home for training. She entered my home just as I was cleaning up from breakfast. I offered her biscuits and gravy, scrambled eggs, and sausage because I had an abundance. She was embarrassed at my offer and only accepted a biscuit, saying that she didn't wish to 'take' from me. I thought how funny her interpretation seemed to me, because I had freely offered and I had plenty!

I explained that I never feel that anyone is taking anything from me, because when I give I always receive back tenfold. My associate expressed a desire to be of this mindset, and, right on cue, my doorbell rang. Standing on my porch was my mom holding a warm, freshly baked loaf of bread. This was immediate proof that a small biscuit had returned to me a large loaf of bread (roughly ten times the size of a biscuit). I am sure my business associate never forgot the lesson.

Creating Abundance

To understand how to create abundance, we must first know exactly what creation is. Without becoming too philosophical or theological, may I suggest that for the purposes of our discussion, that creation is not creatio ex nihilo, an old religious concept

"Giving creates space for something new to come in. The laws of perpetual abundance that the earth was created to sustain, demand we receive back more than we give."

that God created the universe out of nothing.

Nor is creation the newer scientific theory embodied in the Big Bang Theory, that an explosion just happened and everything coincidentally fell in the right place.

I suggest that we begin our discussion on the common ground that anything we can create within our sphere of existence is better termed organized. We reach out and organize from available materials. That's how houses are built, smartphones are made, and babies are created. We organize our relationships, our calendars, our vacations, our experiences. We create, not out of nothingness, but from a world full of resources. We reach out and organize those resources into something meaningful that serves our purposes. Even when I create an art piece like a painting or a quilt, I am using materials that have already been created, like fabric, paint and canvases. We merely order them into something that transforms our imaginations into physical reality.

The Snow Globe Principle

Let's think about how this applies in our lives. I think of it in terms of something I call the Snow Globe Principle. When I shake a snow globe, thousands of little particles of snow begin to flow in every direction. The snow represents matter or materials to work with, but it is disorganized and chaotic. To create order of the disorganized, focus on individual snowflakes. Decide which ones can be organized into something desired. It is important to allow the unneeded pieces to fall away to the ground. We ignore them once we have selected the parts we want. When we focus on those useful parts, and utilize and organize them, we create what we desire with what we have selected from life.

Caution—those who have not yet developed a sense of abundance will look around and try to grab for recognizable and comfortable shapes and images from their past. Seeing the snowflakes through their scarcity filter blinds them to different shaped snowflakes (opportunities) that surround them. They will take what they are used to and force them into familiar patterns. This is not creation, but merely re-building the same comfort zone of the past. This would be like cutting the pieces of a quilt apart with the intention of creating something new. And re-sewing them back together in exactly the same pattern. Even if the pieces are organized into a different pattern, it is basically the same quilt.

To be truly creative, we must learn to donate or sell the old quilt and reach out for new elements that resonate with the new desires we currently feel. Organizing those new elements in a way that aligns with the person we are becoming is abundance.

As with all new concepts, we cannot usually fully see what we are reaching out for until we bring them into our consciousness. It's like looking for the perfect birthday gift for someone, having no clue what it will be. Yet, when we see it, we know it's right.

Therefore, there is an element of faith within abundance. The initial Gateway of Faith must precede the Gateway of Abundance, because an abundance of new materials only exists outside of our current comfort zone.

Stepping into the abundance that exists outside our comfort zone is like flipping the snow globe upside down on purpose to get the pieces swirling around so we can see what is available. The Gateway of Faith helps us get comfortable with the unknown aspects of creation. This is needed, because you will step into faith over and over again with each new level and each new goal. Uncertainty looms in each new step into the darkness until we shine a light on it.

It is easy to recognize the perfect materials, skills, relationships and opportunities as they show up in reality, because they exist inside our imagined end result. Just like the hunt for the perfect birthday gift, these building blocks of our new creation are the resources that we gravitate toward as we maintain focus on our chosen goal.

The Gateway of Abundance demands that you select only those elements of creation that are yours. Be sure to take only what you need, because the Gateway of Abundance guards against scarcity. Being abundant means that you leave all other elements for others to use in their creations. Hoarding elements and matter does not translate into abundance. Learning this lesson prepares you for the Gateway of Charity that you will soon face.

Another concept that the Snow Globe Principle teaches us is the necessity of shaking up our world occasionally. Shaking up our lives helps us see what elements are available to create something new. We usually cannot see abundance while things lie statically where they have been for years. The act of shaking things up is comparable to an act of destruction, but it is from the chaos of destruction that new creation can begin.

Let's not overthink this one. Destruction is not usually perceived as good. But think of a seed after it's planted, if you watch the process of growth on a time-lapse camera, it looks like the seed is being destroyed before the green leaves appear.

Our lives may be cluttered with some old habits and decisions that should be disassembled and replaced with something better. Obliterating those outdated and overused things in our lives may be exactly what we need to create something new and wonderful—not unlike my old bathrooms during my remodel! We might have to sacrifice what currently provides us with a level of comfort, in order to reorganize or replace it with something that takes us to the next level. Sacrifice is really nothing more than an investment—exchanging something good for something better.

We are only truly living if we are changing and growing. If we don't proactively cause some chaos in our lives to bring about growth, then only a crisis or disaster forced upon us can provide a perfect opportunity for deep connection and growth. Knowing this, I have a core belief that has served me: "I consistently create my own perfect environment for growth by choosing to take a leap of faith into a new level of greatness."

I choose growth in this way, because I really would rather not have an outside source choose how my life gets turned upside down. My belief is that if I deliberately engage in change on a regular basis, I will likely only see those opportunities forced upon me when I have a blind-spot. And that opportunity will come precisely when I am ready to improve. I don't know if this is an absolute truth for everyone, but it serves me well to keep me growing and keep me at peace. I am growing at my consciously chosen pace, rather than having it forced upon me.

THERE is not Enough versus THIS is not Enough

There is a distinction between two concepts that needs addressing: "there is not enough" versus "this is not enough." "There is not enough" reflects an attitude that life simply lacks what is needed. "There is not enough" means that it doesn't exist. It cannot be found because it isn't there. In this scenario, there is no progress, because there is no opportunity.

I can understand some who might have this mindset. Someone who may perhaps have a right to think this could be a starving orphan in a place where orphans struggle to barely stay alive. That orphan may find it impossible to see beyond the daily struggle for food. For this poor child, there may not be a way to rise above that level, because the society the orphan subsists in has no concept of abundance.

Conversely, "this is not enough" is a moment of awareness. It is a moment when we look within our own bundle of resources and determine that we have grown beyond what is currently manifesting in our physical world. It is the moment when a job that was fine six months ago suddenly pales in comparison to the level of skill set we have been developing. It is the moment when an abusive marriage is no longer tolerable. It is the moment when a zero balance in the checkbook is not in alignment with our current definition of abundance.

Both concepts are an awareness of what does or does not exist in our physical world in the moment. The first "there is not enough" is based in scarcity and a lack of self-confidence in creating anything different. The second "this is not enough" is like seeing the world we live in for the first time and suddenly noticing the mediocrity we have been allowing as the norm.

The moment the awareness strikes, we are at the apex of choice. We are standing at the threshold of the Gateway of Abundance, deciding whether we will choose our inner faith to step through into the unknown or whether we will choose what feels safe and known. We can continue living the old way and knowing full well that we are choosing into lack, mediocrity, and misalignment with what we are capable of, or we can choose into a new way and align our outside circumstances with the new way we see ourselves. Choosing to level our circumstances to match the new level of belief and worth we have discovered is a giant leap towards integrity in life and business.

A recognition of misalignment provides a playground to try our wings, increasing our confidence by celebrating small successes. Each small success levels up our self-confidence. One by one, our courageous attempts provide evidence that we are stronger than we thought we were. When this happens, our environment MUST change with our new view of ourselves. Our circumstances MUST align with what we believe. The universe is bound by physical law and it applies to every single one of us.

Those who don't know how to change their beliefs and take action on their inspired next steps may never find evidence of abundance. They may instead choose to lower their opinion of themselves to match their surroundings. Whether we lower our opinion of ourselves or we raise the level of what we allow to match the current accurate opinion of ourselves really doesn't matter. The physical law says they must match.

Let me give you an example. In a moment of awareness, I look around and notice that the furniture around me no longer is in alignment with the person I have become. I can choose to believe one of the two following statements. "The furniture in my apartment is worn and dated. Oh well, I guess I really don't deserve nice things." Or, I can choose this one. "The furniture in my apartment is worn and dated. I think I'll donate it so someone else can enjoy the last few years of service it can still provide. I am excited to see what I can find that does suit me!"

As you are learning, you get to choose your surroundings because you get to choose your beliefs. When you put confidence in your beliefs, you MUST receive the new results that the new beliefs create! Whichever course you choose, your surroundings will always match your opinion of yourself.

"There is not enough" indicates that even if I got all that there is, it would not satisfy the need. Time and money might fit into this category, because even though time and money, like most resources, are infinite (meaning there will always be more), a human's ability to obtain more can seem impossible. With proper stewardship there is abundance. If we don't develop an understanding of proper stewardship, we will create scarcity in our mind and in our circumstances. This is especially true when we go around saying, "there is not enough time or money."

"This is not enough" is merely a temporary condition. As I looked at the bathrooms in my home, I noticed the cracking paint and the outdated tiles and fixtures and said, "This is not enough." This is not what I want. This is not what I need for the purpose I am creating. This doesn't match with who I am. But this can be replaced. I can do something about this. It may take some effort, some creativity, and getting rid of my current circumstances, but it can be remedied!

If you are open to learning the lessons needed to prepare yourself to receive more, then more is available to you. It is your right to have everything that is in alignment with your current beliefs, values and understanding of your worth and value. Make the distinction in your mind between there is not enough and this is not enough. Take inventory regularly, notice your growth, and make a conscious choice to reach beyond your current level when you are noticing a misalignment between your circumstances and who you are becoming. Courageously step through the Gateway of Abundance and draw from the vast pool of resources that already exists everywhere around us to organize them into the life you choose.

The principle of abundance is critical to grasp. If you don't catch this all-important piece, you may choose something that doesn't align with what you feel worthy of. Or you may settle for something that is beneath your privilege and ability to attain. If you are still not convinced of the simplicity and ease of it because all you can see is your lack of resources, begin with gratitude. Find gratitude in what is currently in your stewardship. Most people find that they are vastly and richly blessed beyond imagination. State the obvious, that you have a life of abundance and then receive the fruits that your words bring to you.

Don't forget what you learned in the Gateway of Faith that you are eternally worthy, and deserving of all good things which are right for you. This one principle not only sets in motion the truth of the Gateway of Abundance, but prepares you to see the truth of the Gateway of Charity that will follow Abundance.

Most people do not understand charity. They think charity is giving. The counterfeit of charity being about what we can give, is a result of believing the counterfeit that our value comes from what we do. In both cases the focus is on self. We will dive more into the truth of charity in the next section. I hope you are seeing how believing the counterfeit in one gateway skews your ability to find truth in all the gateways that follow.

I'm not talking just monetary abundance. What about choosing a new love relationship based on who you used to be? Will it last if you are lowering yourself constantly to be with the person who would have aligned with the old you? It will likely feel like you are constantly battling with yourself and your loved one.

Remember, the universe brings you precisely what you are asking for according to your beliefs of what you deserve. Consciously choose based on where you are going, not where you have been. And remember that your Permission Process and choosing new beliefs that speak to the life you want, will automatically invite others to level up with you. You almost never need to leave a situation or relationship. And you never need to confront someone about problems from the past! As you change your beliefs, the universe will provide your desired new scenario in one of three ways:
1. The situation will change to align with the new you.
2. The situation will fall away and you won't have to deal with it.
3. The situation will continue as is and it won't bother you anymore.

I promise that the way the universe provides will be the absolute perfect way for you, according to the beliefs you have chosen into.

That is one of the really cool things about how the universe lines up your life as you approach the end result you are seeking. You don't have to do anything except follow your intuition for your desired life to fall into place. You don't have to ask for a divorce, you don't have to quit your job, you don't have to make your daughter clean up her room. When you notice that something is not enough, just claim what is enough. Choose that, and declare it as yours because it aligns with who you have become.

The universe will provide it—every time! You don't get to choose how, but you can trust that it will be provided in the best possible way. It is always better than you could have planned it out yourself. In the example of your daughter cleaning her room, here is how it might play out.

1. You notice the mess and you become aware that "this is not enough."
2. You declare a clean room is what you desire. You are open to however it comes to you.
3. The universe provides a solution that lines up with your new belief—either she will clean it on her own, someone else (maybe even you) will clean it for her, or perhaps you will realize it is your daughter's space and not yours. If the latter is the case, you may realize you have been forcing your beliefs on your daughter and the messy room all of a sudden may become a lower priority than your relationship with your daughter and it will not bother you anymore.

The way your new belief plays out is perfect and given in the best way possible for the new person you have become. There is never any force, or stress. The evidence of the new belief just comes. How cool is that!

The key is to declare from the space that you have control. You might say, "I love that I live in a clean and orderly home. I value organization. I love the closeness I feel with my family within my home, especially my relationship with my daughter." Most likely, this is really what you are trying to create. Let the Universe provide what you truly want (family and personal harmony), rather than what you think you want (a daughter's clean room).

If you ever find yourself saying "there is not enough," look around and see what you have right at your fingertips. Your old beliefs and expectations of yourself created everything that you currently have in your life. You are an amazing and powerful creator! Express gratitude for all you have and be content that you created it! And then see if you are ready to shift into "this is not enough," which means you are noticing and acknowledging the beauty of the blessings in your life, but also know you are capable of so much more.

Am I Enough?

I think we can say from what we have been discussing that there is always enough. But I recognize that the reality of not having enough may come up quite often. Perhaps this may lead to the core of all limiting beliefs: "I am not enough." This belief can be fueled by overwhelming evidence that I have not yet accomplished what I set out to do. I keep saying there is enough, but my credit cards are still maxed out. Or maybe I am getting negative feedback from a well-meaning (or not so well-meaning) relative or friend about my current relationship. What then?

I cannot stress enough that "I am not enough" is the most destructive belief there is. It makes us powerless to change. If I am not enough, there is no program, mentor, God or Savior who can change that. This belief will not only sabotage your chances at success, it will strip you of self-worth. It will sentence you to a mediocre life, relying on the pity of others for your survival. Debt and scarcity will be your constant companions with no hope of freeing yourself. Success will be short-lived and the devastating losses that are sure to follow will crush you.

Know this! YOU ARE ENOUGH. You are always enough in the present moment with what you know. If the lesson you get when you have a perceived failure is "I am not enough" you got the wrong lesson. That is never the lesson and that is never the truth. Just as there is enough for everyone's creations, you are enough for your creation. You are a loved being with divine parentage and eternal worth. You have always existed, and the frailties of human existence change none of that.

The truth that there is enough encompasses the entire planet and the universe. There is an abundance of all needful and desirable things. We will never run out of materials that are available for our particular creations. We are each creating something unique. There is no competition or shortage of resources. There is enough to go around because we are all seeking something unique to us.

Even "This is enough" is a temporary state of being. It is enough for now. There will come a time when my mind envisions something greater, and what I accept of myself will be greater than it is today. When that moment arrives, the reality of mediocrity will set in. At that time, I get to choose again. I can choose to grow or I can choose to stagnate. And please understand that growth is a basic need for all humans. If I choose to continually grow, I will need to shake up the snow globe, let some old things go, and reach out and gather in different matter to create what I desire at that time. I am enough to do my part. The plan that emerges will be enough, until I have prepared myself to receive something more.

The message of the Gateway of Abundance is that I am content through every stage and I am loving everything that is. The energy that fuels my continual growth is love for my own growth and love for those I can serve as I become more self-actualized. The message is never the scarcity that accompanies, "I am not enough and I have to keep achieving to prove that I am."

If I were in a perpetual state of this is enough, I would severely limit my own growth. I would limit my ability to make more, love more, and do more with my life. I am not done with living until my time is up here on earth, so I should always be growing, as living things do. As a result, I should never feel like my life is enough for extended periods of time. I choose to live; therefore, I choose to grow at a steady pace.

Each of us strives to become the person we envision ourselves to be, and when we become that person, we celebrate. Because we are then free to look outside of ourselves and help those around us to discover their greatness. When I'm no longer focused on me, I can focus on things outside of myself. In the next gateway, you will understand more about the power of focusing on others as a means of creating more ease and efficiency in your manifesting process.

Allow me to share one final simple example of how the Gateway of Abundance served me. It was in one of those moments that I was looking around my house one day and noticed an old chair. This chair was missing a leg and had scribbling on the back from one of the children long ago. I said, "That old chair has to go...NOW!" What I meant was "That old chair is not enough!" I had changed; I was no longer the person who had broken furniture in her home. Therefore, the chair had to go. The chair was no longer enough, because it was out of alignment with the person I was at that moment.

So I deliberately picked up the snow globe and shook it. I had identified an item that was blocking me from receiving new, available space and materials, and I began to re-create my environment by giving it away.

My daughter's boyfriend graciously carried the chair up the stairs and directly outside to the bed of my pickup truck. We immediately took it to a second-hand store where I am sure someone with great do-it-yourself skills discovered it and is now enjoying it in their home with a new leg and a beautiful slipcover. While I was standing in the second-hand store, I saw the perfect chair (a beautiful snowflake swirling in the snow globe) that had just been delivered from someone else's home. I claimed it as my next piece of furniture that was enough.

Am I too good for second hand furniture? Nope. The chair I got rid of simply didn't fit me anymore. By holding onto it after I knew it no longer belonged to me, I would have been hoarding matter in someone else's snow globe. The chair I found that day was donated as matter in my own snow globe.

I acted immediately when I felt inspired to give away my chair. And because I acted immediately, I found the perfect replacement at the second-hand store. If I had told myself that the chair would do for another couple years I probably would still have the scribbled on, old gold, 1970's-style, easy chair with the broken leg. I wouldn't have been in the right place at the right time to claim my new chair.

Abundance is a state of enough and being content with that—having enough, doing enough, and being enough. It does not mean you cannot add to what you have or what you are. If the wealthiest person in the world declared, "I am the wealthiest person in the world, and it is enough," then that person could go out and work another six months and come away with even more wealth than ever before. Likewise, the best-educated person in the world can arrive at a point in life where the level of education is enough, and then, by different means, continue to learn more and more. Declaring that something is enough is not to say that we are done and cannot receive anymore. It is an expression of gratitude and peace that regardless of circumstance, we are and have enough.

"What if the glass were not half empty or half full, but simply...enough?"- Kevin Clayson

Our attitude of enough is what allowed my husband and me to be able to pay all our monthly obligations when he became disabled, even in the situation of a consistent $1,800 monthly deficit. Regardless of circumstance, there can be enough.

Are you beginning to see how intertwined the gateways are? The deliberate efforts you give in one gateway will liberate you to be more genuine in the next. The wisdom you gain within this Gateway of Abundance will prepare you to see and more readily embrace the truth of the gateways that follow.

Your Rite of Passage through the Gateway of Abundance
How Aligned Are You with Abundance?

Evaluate yourself on a scale of 1-5 (5 is completely aligned):
1. I give in a way that also serves me. By giving something that no longer belongs to me, I am creating space for receiving something that aligns with who I am today. I give to start the process and flow of abundance. (You will learn in the next gateway, the Gateway of Charity what you should give.)
2. I believe there is enough--enough for everyone to have what they desire. Because this is an absolute truth, it is easy to be generous. I know that helping you doesn't diminish what I receive and achieve.
3. I believe this is enough. I am content with what has been created so far. When I outgrow this, my realization that this is no longer enough becomes my springboard for creating more of what I desire at my current level of achievement and becoming.
4. I believe I am enough. When the time comes that I feel it's time to level up, I am still enough. I am just seeing that my potential is not yet met. I embrace a vision of a better me, and I courageously become that improved version of myself. I believe all along that I am enough to achieve it.

The Seven Gateways

MILEPOST 2 - CHOOSING TO LOVE

In the weeks that followed, I threw myself into searching for the next perfect opportunity that might guarantee a fulfilling career with a financially stable future for my family. After all, I am a talented, independent leader capable of creating a successful outcome wherever I land...right?

The next position I secured was in management, a manufacturing company where I was supervising the shipping department. Again, I dove in with fierce loyalty and whole-hearted commitment to the company.

As always, I claimed ownership of my space and even sent an email to the owner after just a couple of weeks at my new job, asking what his mission for the company was (so that I could support it in some way through the work we were doing in my shipping department).

The morning after my email was delivered in his inbox, the owner walked into my office and shut the door behind him. I was surprised, though grateful. I felt honored that he would answer my email so promptly, and in person. But the response was not what I expected. The first words out of his mouth painted a clear picture that there was no mission, no vision or cause that I could get behind, at least as far as I was concerned.

"How DARE you email me!" He spat. "You have a supervisor. If you have a question, you email your supervisor. And as for your mission," he loudly continued, "you SHIP things! That is all you do. You SHIP things!" And he promptly turned and strode out of my office before I could even think of what to say.

I sat for several moments with my mouth open, but speechless.

I resolved that if I didn't have permission to contribute to the mission of the company, I could at least change the atmosphere and energy of my department and be a stellar example of efficiency in my little corner. I even had the fairy tale dream that I could change the morale of the entire company beginning with me. "If you want to see a change, begin with the person in the mirror." That is how the saying goes.

I saw greatness in my team. I was complimentary of every success and together we were determined to make work fun. I was committed to making the changes that gave all of us the best chance for success. Each individual on my team had a unique set of skills. I saw their talents and I assigned the tasks that best suited them. We were thriving.

We were thriving. But then my supervisors began micromanaging my department. I couldn't understand it. We worked so well together when left alone, what reason could they possibly have for interfering? I received memos occasionally, and then daily, about new policies and changes I was expected to implement. The requests became ridiculous to the point that they began to conflict with each other. I could no longer lead my area, and my stellar team began to fall behind.

I continued at that job several more months, doing my best to toe the line, before finally being fired. The day before I was let go, I received tasks from three separate supervisors. Each one alone could not be humanly performed in the time allotted. I felt defeated.

What could possibly have gone wrong? Normally, I am great at systemizing and delegating to get the job done with excellence. My supervisors love me. I could not explain the rapid loss of trust I had felt from those above me.

My only explanation was that somehow I was getting it wrong. I felt that I must not be as smart as I thought I was. I was obviously not management material, and most certainly was not CEO material. I began to question my worth.

Even more painful than being escorted from the building, final paycheck in hand, was the realization that a pattern was once again repeating itself - the pattern of dedicating my best, throwing my heart into building something meaningful, only to be disappointed and finally cast aside.

The Seven Gateways

THE THIRD GATEWAY- CHARITY

The Counterfeit

I saw my own potential and was attempting to make things better by taking ownership of my position. My supervisor forbade me from even communicating my desires to help the team succeed. In that business culture, it was not my place to force change. I had one task, but to do my best, I felt I had to overstep my bounds. The counterfeit of The Gateway of Charity is that for me to be fulfilling my potential, I have to help others be their best. It is my duty to make sure that others are successful, even if it costs me my own authenticity.

The Truth

Charity is the pure love of Christ. I see myself and others through the eyes of God. I recognize their divine genius and I recognize my own divine genius. I serve in the way I best contribute, and I expect others to serve in the way they best contribute. I offer my value in places where it is received and appreciated and I do not tolerate remaining in a space where I am not allowed to contribute my best. I seek out others who have value that I appreciate. We each are given space to create authentically within our own gifts and we build a complete team of individual talent.

The counterfeit is a lose/lose. Both the creator and the one supporting the creation miss the value that could be exchanged. Both sacrifice what they could receive if it were a perfect fit. The truth is a win/win. Both receive more than they give and they rise together.

My Assessment

I am creating in a place that is out of alignment with my values and core beliefs. I accept the first management position that comes along because I am desperate. Then, I remain at a job that is fundamentally wrong for me because I have turned inward on myself. I am looking for the reason I am not being successful, rather than recognizing that neither I, nor my supervisors have charity.

It becomes an inner game—I make the decision that I AM a disappointment, rather than life or my job is a disappointment. It is not my circumstances that are bad; it is me that is bad. I do not have charity for myself.

The lesson is never, "I am not good enough." My lesson should have been, "I don't belong here. I don't fit."

My natural leadership style is to find the good in people and help them excel within their natural gifts. I encourage them to take ownership of their responsibilities individually and work together as a team. I am out of alignment with the way this particular company is run. In trying to be me, I cause friction in the following ways:

1. I make the other managers look bad. Employees begin requesting to be moved to my area. Those in my department are the only happy people in the entire company. It becomes critical that I be shut down to avoid an uprising. I really am making a difference, but not the kind that would be tolerated in a company that relies on fear to gain employee loyalty.
2. I don't need a supervisor. We were capable of working well independently. In a fear-based environment it is absolutely necessary that everyone knows what everyone else is doing. Since I don't need to be motivated to do a good job, micro-

managing is introduced so that there are constant checks and balances. I don't do well conforming to the normal system, so the fear is turned back on the one who is out of alignment with the system. Their fear can only be resolved by eliminating the enemy...me.

Entering the Gateway of Charity

Society's definition of charity comes from the counterfeit that neither I nor you is inherently valuable. It comes from the belief that we are all flawed in some way and need to be fixed. Somewhere along the way there is a decision that I have more, so I should give to those less abundant. You have more, so you should give of your abundance to me. There is a decision that someone is "less than."

Add to that, our desire to follow our perfect example, Jesus Christ in his ministry. The counterfeit here is that we must be the savior. The truth is that Jesus Christ saw himself through God's eyes and knew the contribution he could make. If you really study Christ's miracles, you will find that he passed many people by. Even when he was petitioned, he asked, "do you have the faith to be healed?" He qualified the recipient before he offered his gift. And so should we.

It has been said that charity is the pure love of Christ, the pure love that He has for each individual soul. To see ourselves through His eyes is to see infinite worth and value.

This is the true definition of charity, to see within ourselves and in others the vitally important worth and
value we are capable of contributing. If we try to give from our own abundance, it will eventually be depleted. If we give from the pure love of Christ, whose abundance is described as living water that is ever flowing, the source is limitless.

The only reason we would give of our abundance to another, would be when we discern, as Christ did, that our own contribution would be received, appreciated, and valued equal to the value Christ places on it. The only reason we would ask another to contribute their abundance would be when we discern that their value is vitally important to our own creation. In this way, exchanging value within the truth of charity, both are lifted and increased together through the infinite source of abundance. There is a realization that we all come to at some point on

"But charity is the pure love of Christ, and it endureth forever; and whoso is found possessed of it at the last day, it shall be well with him." -Moroni 7:47, The Book of Mormon

our path: I cannot do it all alone. We all learn that in order to influence those around us and realize our full potential, we need others to be involved in our process. We need synergy. Synergy is chemistry. Combining the right amounts of individual genius produces exponential results that could not be created separately.

Leverage Becomes Love

Stephen Covey, the author of *The Seven Habits of Highly Effective People* has been quoted as saying, "Synergy is the highest activity of life; it creates new untapped alternatives; it values and exploits the mental, emotional and psychological differences between people."

The word 'exploit' caught my attention in the above quote by Stephen Covey. I believe most people give this word a negative connotation; conversely, many people would assign a positive connotation to the word synergy. How can one be used to describe the other if one is negative and the other positive?

"Synergy is not the same as compromise. In a compromise, one plus one equals one and a half at best." -Dr. Stephen R. Covey

I am going to explain by giving you a lesson in opposition. Originally when I received the Gateway of Charity, I called it the Gateway of Leverage, a word that could be perceived as negative when associated with utilizing other people and resources. As this gateway evolved I saw an interesting connection between leverage and love (which I now refer to as charity).

I asked more questions and received more information and I now understand on a deeper level what true charity means and how it works as leverage. Leveraging others' skills and talents is true charity. Let me explain my thinking.

In including others in our goals and achievements, they bring their time, talents, efforts, and insights to our creation process. The gifts they offer save us trial and possibly more error than is necessary. Each of us is uniquely gifted, but we are also each lacking in some way—we are lacking in a gift that has been mastered by another.

My husband and I are a great team because he is solid and stalwart with our financial game plan, and I believe anything is possible. I alone would probably be bankrupt; he alone would be bored with life. We might both achieve financial independence eventually, but together we arrive at our destination faster and with the least number of bruises. All the while, we feel extreme gratitude for one another's strengths that have helped us reach our goals.

Alone I cannot possibly have everything necessary to complete a project in the most efficient and worthwhile way. Of course, I can do it all myself and do a fine job, but if I combine the strengths of others with my own, no energy is wasted, more perspectives are seen, life is more interesting because there are more personalities to mix things up. Ultimately everyone benefits! By asking others to step in with their gifts and give their all, I am leveraging them for my benefit and theirs.

Leverage can sometimes be viewed as a negative. An example of a counterfeit of leverage when it comes to people, is when a boss tells his/her employee to work for the employer's success and the employee is only getting a paycheck out of it. Similar to my experience shared above, this management style produces employees that lack drive and self-worth. It is a destructive way of utilizing the valuable principle of leverage. Remember in the Gateway of Abundance we learned that we are enough and we have value.

The words may be different, but many times I observe people behaving in this way with their kids, their co-workers, their spouse, or their clients. Even if the words aren't spoken, the energy is that of only tolerating people for

"Money is a by-product of giving value. It is not the reason we give."

the sake of getting ahead or building your own dream.

The type of leverage that is created from this approach is more like manipulation. You can definitely have huge success when you use others to help you become wealthy and successful. But at the end of the day, what you attract into your life is equal to the value you give out.

Giving value to others in a way that also gives me what I value is the way to bring abundance into my life. If I am serving someone else simply for a paycheck, it is not serving me. Unless the work I am doing is nourishing to my soul or fulfilling my purpose in some way, I will eventually lose interest if it is only for money.

If we can see a gift inside a person and invite them to show up in service to us in that way, we are not only serving ourselves, we are serving them. They are paid because they serve in a way they are gifted, but it is not in money. Their paycheck is using and strengthening their talents and gifts. We are creating a space for them to serve in their talent. The highest compliment and opportunity you can give a person is a space to be useful in a way that feels equally beneficial for them.

In this type of environment, the motivation to do a good job is ever-present. They are motivated by love, not fear. And it is a love for themselves, not for building someone else's empire.

Holding a paycheck or position over someone's head, is fear motivation and it will only work in the short-term. Even expecting someone to show up to work in their fullest, most gifted capacity for your benefit becomes a joy for them, when they are equally benefited. And that is why after just a few days of contemplation of this new gateway, I changed the name from the Gateway of Leverage, to the Gateway of Charity.

Charity is the pure love of Christ. In other words, charity is seeing another through Christ's eyes. Christ was really good at seeing someone in their purest, most perfect form, and inviting them to live up to it.

If we are truly being charitable, we wouldn't hire someone because they needed a job. The only reason we would hire someone, is because they can bring something more to our organization and our dreams than we currently can do without them. This perpetuates the cycle of abundance that we have already learned through the Gateway of Abundance. Inviting others to give and serve in the way they are gifted, perpetuates the cycle of abundance for themselves as well as for us.

We are leveraging their skills for our benefit as well as theirs, because we have identified a need we have, and we have seen that they can fill it. We have seen how they can increase synergistically, the outcome of our goals, and we want the shortest gestation period possible. So they are critical to our fastest, most efficient positive outcome.

If I am not digging deep within my soul and finding the very best I am capable of giving, I am not fully participating in the Gateway of Abundance for myself. At the same time, I am limiting the amount of value I can receive in return. I can only expect a return of what I am giving out. If I am expecting the best of those I invite into my service, it is imperative that I am giving my best. The old saying "do as I say, not as I do" doesn't sit well when inviting others in to serve us in creating a synergistic result.

Finding my own gifts and expressing myself fully through them, while inviting others who are gifted in ways I am not, to stand fully in their gifts as we create together is the most authentic way to experience and invite others to begin understanding the Gateway of Charity.

When I first starting employing the Gateway of Charity in my life, I would create leverage by finding people who were good at things I wasn't particularly good at. I would employ their talents and utilize their skills, and together we could work synergistically to accomplish tasks that were far beyond our own limited abilities. We worked together on my business, projects and dreams.

I was actually giving them the opportunity to grow and realize their own full potential by providing a safe training ground where they could practice doing what they loved. When I came to this understanding—that by inviting them to support me I was helping then to feel fulfilled and happy, I finally understood that this form of human interaction and giving service and opportunities was simply loving in the highest way possible. I am working with others, seeing them in their highest and best selves, and inviting them to step up into their highest potential to create something wonderful with me.

The creation of a community to accomplish a common goal, something that each member could not have accomplished alone, is synergistic, and it leverages the abilities of each member exponentially. This is the Gateway of Charity. When we allow others to share a piece of themselves in a common undertaking by bringing their lives' experiences and abilities to the job in a passionate way, we create an opportunity for real fulfillment for others and for ourselves.

Think about a project you've worked on, that was not very fun. The sharing of the burden with others, some who had greater ability or passion than you, and therefore, a happier outlook on the tasks at hand, may have increased your level of satisfaction during the project. As you watched them enthusiastically throw their hearts into the work, you may have been motivated to give more than you originally desired to give.

This is true in my experience. I have a dear great-aunt who had a deep love for family history. Due to an eye disorder, she couldn't tell if a line was perfectly horizontal or slanted. She hired me when I was 15 years old to typeset and place photos in a huge book she created about our family. Prior to this summer job, you couldn't have paid me to do family history--that was for old people. But in working with her, seeing her enthusiastic dedication to the work, and experiencing first-hand the spiritual connection she felt with our ancestors, I grew to love not only my ancestors as real people, but I also grew to love family history as well. I offered my young, sharp eyes; she offered her expertise and knowledge of family history. Together we fulfilled a life mission for her and I found greater joy and fulfillment as I became part of her mission.

An additional aspect of the Gateway of Charity is allowing others to share the burdens of the common task.

As we distribute the weight of the burden, we find that there are no catastrophic failures for the whole.

It is in the mutual support and sharing of opportunities and burdens that humans grow both individually and together. This is most likely why people bond during a natural disaster. We can manufacture that kind of environment on purpose every day in a business or in a family by giving our all and inviting others to do the same.

> *"Many people want to be paid more and do less... the concept of wanting to work less and be paid more ultimately makes everyone poorer, regardless of the amount of money they earn."*
> *-Robert Kiyosaki, Unfair Advantage*

An important part of the Gateway of Charity is learning to do more than just give of yourself. It is important to give yourself away. The Gateway of Abundance teaches that we each will receive equal or greater than what we give. To receive more, we must be willing to give more.

Giving Yourself Away

We give ourselves away through our strengths and talents. We are not giving something we have; we are giving a piece of us. We are giving our hearts. When we do this, we invite others to do the same, empowering them to feel the benefits of abundance in their lives (giving in a way that also immediately pays them, and giving them a sense of their innate worth).

Once you start giving yourself away, in an authentic way that also serves you, it gets under your skin. The innate need to love and serve others is such a strong desire in each of us that when we get a taste of it, we begin seeing the greatness in others everywhere. As a result, all aspects of our lives change, and we fill our lives and the lives of our family members and associates with charity, the highest form of love. There can be no greater gift, so in effect you are asking the universe to reciprocate with the greatest gifts it has to offer you.

But if I give myself away, won't I eventually have nothing left to give? That is the crazy part...the more authentically we give, the more positive energy we generate, the more fuel we add to our passions. The only time we become depleted is when we give unwillingly or in a way that feels inauthentic.

Try this exercise next time you are asked to volunteer. Check in with yourself and ask these questions: Does this opportunity align with my purpose and my natural strengths? Am I moved by my passion to jump at this opportunity? If the answer is 'no,' write your name down anyway. Then see how you feel from that moment until the volunteering is over. Even beyond that, how many times do you feel regret for following through with the assignment. Just try it, and you will understand what I mean when I say that serving in the wrong way depletes you.

Giving and Receiving

It may not yet be completely obvious why the Gateway of Charity comes after the Gateway of Abundance. Let me help you see how this works in real life. In the Gateway of Abundance, we have a greater awareness of all the options and materials available to us. We begin to believe that whatever we choose is possible.

It could become overwhelming if we see so many opportunities but ascertain that we are all alone in our journey. If we believe we have to figure it all out and do everything ourselves, it would not be humanly possible to accomplish everything required to reach even one goal, let alone take advantage of all the options available.

Also remember the new wisdom gathered concerning abundance. When we give in a way that serves us, we are already being paid. We are already receiving when we give in a way that fulfills the soul.

These two principles alone—seeing all the possibilities and choosing abundance by giving in a way that gives back to us—gives us reason enough to really want to invite others to use their gifts by becoming part of our talented team. Seeing others in their highest and best capacity and expecting them to show up fully in that way epitomizes the Gateway of Charity. The energy that this type of invitation carries with it is interpreted as generosity and people are naturally drawn to want to be part of what we are building.

Seeing the Best in Others

I am sure you have experienced this yourself. When others see the beauty and gifts in you, you naturally rise to their expectation. This is called the Pygmalion Effect. Some call it Self-fulfilling prophecy. High vibration words, thoughts, and beliefs attract high vibration energy. You cannot give out one thing and get something else in return. Just as the Gateway of Abundance invites good karma, our purely honest beliefs about someone's potential will invite them to be that!

We can help people see their highest and best selves when we invite them to live at a higher level. But there is a specific way to do this that lovingly helps them rise to this elevated plane. The counterfeit of inviting others into their highest self would be to ask questions like, "What is wrong with you? You are smarter than that!" This is not inviting people to show up in their divinity. A more authentic method encourages others to see themselves at their best and become the most they can be. One way to do this is to share observations about their choices in a positive manner, possibly commenting with "That's an interesting choice. That really is unlike you." This helps the person recognize that you see who they really are and gives them pause to look at why they did what they did, and correct it if they choose.

In some cases, the emotional investment we make in others can seem taxing at times. However, the Gateway of Abundance dictates that there is enough love in every situation. There is always enough. The Gateway of Charity lies just beyond the Gateway of Abundance. When you really understand and embrace abundance, you are on your way to living a Gateway of Charity.

Does giving love mean that we must let others make their choices at the expense of ours? I will answer that question in a way that the Gateway of Charity has helped me understand it. Love also applies to me. I love myself so much that I receive only what serves me.

Some relationships are abusive. The kind of giving that takes your own happiness out of the equation, serves neither the person giving nor the person receiving. Therefore, there is no abundance created on either side.

In these types of relationships, it is still important to love. We can continue to love others by seeing their greatness, whether they are displaying it or not. And we can continue to love ourselves enough to be in integrity with what we believe is in alignment with our divine spirit (our highest and best).

Some choose to put walls around themselves, walls that would shut out the possibility of hurt and pain. These same walls, however, tend to also shut in. Creating a barrier gives some a feeling of safety against a possible confrontation. They set up a protective energetic shield so that when people show up a certain way they can keep the energy at arm's length. I choose a different tactic. Rather than boundaries, I set standards that align with my purpose and values. A standard, as a flag, can be seen for miles around. Before someone ever reaches me, they already know the person I am and what I will accept in my space. For example, if someone is looking for a scapegoat or victim, they will look elsewhere because my energy is not attracting them. On the other hand, if I carry around a belief that I will be hurt, I cannot stop hurt from coming!

By setting a standard of respect for myself and expectation that others will respect me as well, the vibration that emanates from me is that of a confident respected being, not a victim. Therefore, I never even have to interact with those who are seeking a victim. The law of attraction demands that we get what we ask for, so I choose my standards and act according to the standards I set. If I have a standard of respect, I give out nothing but respect and I expect nothing but respect in return. The energetic vibration of respect emanates from me, so there is never a confrontation of disrespect where I am concerned.

We can love others in the highest way, seeing them as God sees them, and we can maintain our own standards and love ourselves, even while others show up however they choose.

Are you beginning to see that you have control?

The Gateway of Charity shows us how to give, in the way that serves us best, and it shows us how to receive from others, in the way that serves them best. To receive from others is to leverage their skills for mutual advantage. Perfect partnerships will emerge as we think, believe, and act in perfect alignment with our own purposes. Natural energetic attractions will happen when we love and see ourselves and others beyond surface actions.

Another aspect of the Gateway of Charity is that each of us is so unique in our purpose that there is no competition. I can invite you to participate in what I am creating with no worry or fear that you will steal my clients or my ideas, because only I can be me, in the way that I can be me. No other person can duplicate and use my gifts in quite the same way I do. As a result, I can give myself fully and freely, without fear.

Being Paid for Your Gifts

This naturally leads to the discussion of being paid well for our products and services. Many feel that their gifts are so sacred or priceless that there really is no price they can ask. Therefore, many don't ask for any compensation. They feel it is a gift from God and charging to share this gift doesn't honor Him or the gift.

I invite you to look beyond money. I have found that money is a byproduct of fully giving myself and sharing my value. Since I am giving fully and freely, it seems natural to expect my client to reciprocate. But my client is not giving me money, he is giving me hours of work at his place of employment. In our world, money is an acceptable form of value exchange. It is the one thing we can all agree on where value is concerned. Money is a byproduct of my client showing up fully for his boss. Money is a byproduct of me showing up fully for my client. We agree on the value that is being exchanged for my gift, and we agree on the value that is being exchanged for his gift.

We use money because it is simpler to say, "That is worth $45.00" than, "That is worth 1.25 hours of work at your place of employment." We both know that 1.25 hours is worth $45.00. Time, energy, commitment to get up and go to work every morning, these are really what he is trading for what he is asking of me. He is actually giving me his talent and gift if he is working at a place that supports him living his purpose.

This is the only fair exchange. Because we are giving our sacred gift, it is only fair that they are giving theirs. Every person in every culture uses a form of money to represent this exchange so it is more universal. Otherwise, we would be constantly evaluating how much a gift is worth. As has been expressed earlier, you cannot put a price on that.

When one person gives more than they receive (or receives more than they give), an unhealthy relationship develops. I worked for a doctor years ago and did everything for him except examine patients. Even then, I did much to prepare the patient so that when he entered the room, the patient already trusted him and felt completely secure in having him examine them. When I left my position in his office, it felt awkward. The value I was giving was so far above the pay I was receiving that the relationship was out of balance. I had created a relationship where I was entitled to a tremendous amount of value. I was being paid much less. So when I told him I was leaving, it felt like a servant rebelling against a master. I had created a form of bondage in the guise of relationship debt. This is never a happy situation. And it is nearly impossible to balance the budget when this type of debt is created. In order to avoid this, give freely, give fully, and ask and expect your clients and all relationships to do the same. And because money is our universal form of exchange, it is easiest to receive payment in cash.

Therefore, as we offer ourselves and our gifts to others, we must ask the same of them in return. If we wish to assist someone else in becoming something greater than they currently are, we must see their greatness and expect them to express their greatness fully and freely. We lift ourselves in the act of lifting others, and vice versa.

This is part of the reciprocity effect of abundance and charity. But always remember that the Gateway of Abundance, closely followed by the Gateway of Charity begins with me. I must give in a way that immediately fuels and satisfies me. Furthermore, as I see a gift in another that supports me, I must be willing to invite them to give to me with the same whole-hearted energy.

Taking this a little closer to home, a breakdown in abundance results when I am working at a job I hate or that doesn't fulfill me. There is a deficit of value. Remember, the money I give to others is not money, it is my time, my energy and my gifts I am giving my employer.

If I hate my job, in essence I have no value to give, in fact I have less than zero value to offer because I am wishing I could be somewhere else when I am at work. The value with which I am paying for all my goods and services is hate, regret, distraction and wishful thinking. I may be providing value to my employer, but I am not taking any value with me when I leave each day.

This scenario is the epitome of relationship debt with me getting ripped off every day. And it's not the employer's fault. I choose my attitude about how that job is serving my purpose. I can either change my perspective and find some reason why this job does fulfill a part of my purpose, or is at least a stepping stone, or I can change my job. Either choice will put me back into the flow of positive abundance.

> *"I am only one, but I am one. I cannot do everything, but I can do something."*
> -Edward Everett Hale

In a perfect world, everyone would give value in a way that fulfills their individual purpose. And others would give their value to receive what you have to offer. You can create this perfect world in your own life by only offering your time, energy and gifts to causes that you love and value. To be in balance, it is absolutely imperative to your flow of abundance that you are paid for what you love and value.

Giving ourselves away creates a space for receiving, yet when we give in this way, there is no hole to fill. Immediately when we give, we are filled to overflowing. And the person who receives our gift is motivated to give fully as well. In this way, we can never outgive anyone. Abundance literally is added upon each time something is given away.

Just as one seed creates thousands or millions of pieces of fruit over a lifetime, my one tiny gift to mankind produces a ripple effect that cannot be measured, diminished or destroyed.

Take Action and Invite with Sincerity

I cannot wait for others to step up and begin the process. No one can gift me abundance or charity. I lead the way. The giving begins from within. I must initiate it. There is no abundance if I tell others they must give a little or if I give half-heartedly. I start the process by giving myself completely in commitment and unprecedented free expression. Only then am I perceived as credible enough to invite others to support my cause.

Now that you see that you are the catalyst for your own abundance, what are you waiting for? Who are you inspired to serve today? In what way can you serve that pays you at the same time?

People will move if we prod them—fear, hunger, poverty, threats, even enticing with rewards are all motivators to push someone along—but a rite of passage through a gateway is something quite different. It is a conscious choice. Are you ready to invite others in to help boost your abundance—and theirs—by leveraging their gifts? If the answer is yes, you are ready to walk through the Gateway of Charity.

Being crystal clear of your own vision of the end result you are communicating is what garners trust from those who might choose in. Thus, your faith in your own cause is required. Even before you are absolutely sure of its successful outcome, faith invites the relationship capital that is needed to complete the picture—your faith invites people to buy into your vision and to buy into you. Your willingness to share your vision with others demonstrates that you are not threatened or fearful of losing your competitive edge. This open invitation communicates abundance and that is highly attractive. You radiate the energy of abundance because it is a skill you learned prior to the Gateway of Charity.

The invitation to support my cause cannot be done with selfish motives or for accolades or social rewards. Giving my best and anticipating (but not demanding) that others will do the same is the free space where authentic creation takes place. By giving me the best of you just as I am giving you the best of me, magic happens. More is created together than could be created individually. That is abundance. This works in any relationship or partnership—work, marriage, volunteer committee, and parenting.

This mutual service, freely given to one another, is the root of the Gateway of Charity. Because it is synergistic and produces phenomenal results, you may understand why I thought of this gateway as a means of leverage initially. When I more fully appreciated the aspect of what was being leveraged, I could only feel gratitude and respect of what was being offered—the person's highest and best as a resource for my purpose.

The Gateway of Charity is more than just me leveraging them, as is so often the case in an employee/employer situation where someone is just working for money. They are also leveraging me as a setting where they can play in their passion! As I let them see their own reflection in my expression of gratitude for their worth and contribution, and as I see the same in the intensity they bring with their talents, a safe place for both of us to leap to the next level is established and a synergistic partnership is the result.

Sometimes it is hard to see our own greatness, even when reflected by another. For instance, I invariably see the potential in my mentoring clients long before they can see it in themselves. This is often because they don't believe that what they see reflected is true for them. They have too many experiences that have led them to believe they are not that great. The challenge, then, is to clear the fog of the limiting beliefs that are hindering their sight so they can see their greatness, too.

Convicting Evidence of Value

Allow me to share an example of the Gateway of Charity and the effect it can have on an otherwise doomed life. I facilitated a class every week sponsored by the local jail for a group of inmates who were currently on parole. These people were ordered by the court to check in once a week for a drug test and to attend my class each Monday as part of their rehabilitation.

I learned quickly as I interacted with the students that they had learned to protect themselves while in jail or possibly in their home environment prior to jail by not displaying any weakness or vulnerability. Most weeks, a new group of individuals would come in, making a conscious effort not to look anyone in the eye, not divulging any information other than the required, and definitely not participating by sharing their innermost thoughts and feelings.

One young man sat in the back of the classroom with his chair tipped against the wall and his hat pulled down shadowing his eyes. At first, he just appeared to be present in body only and otherwise wished to be somewhere else entirely. However, he eventually began to join in the conversations, offering comments from his seat in the back. He rarely tipped his hat back and many times it was difficult to even know who had spoken because he spoke from under the bill of his hat.

I believe that at the time he didn't want to admit to himself (or let on to others) that he was that interested in improving his life by incorporating the skills we were discussing. But his comments were reflecting the principles I was teaching, and I could tell that he was trying to incorporate the principles into his broken life. It was apparent that it was hard for him to believe that the truths he was learning could actually apply to him. I perceived that he was actually developing a substantial understanding of the precepts; his comments betrayed a deeper interest than he let on.

I could tell that this young man felt alone, and that there was little support in the world for him or "someone like him" as I once heard him say. Although he didn't specifically ask, he was crying out for help.

I wasn't sure that he was feeling safe enough in class to open up with his feelings, so after a few weeks I approached him and asked if he could remain after class for a while. He explained he could stay until it was time for him to leave for his job, about 40 minutes after class. For the next several weeks, until his sentence had been served, we could be found after class sitting in a couple of chairs in the hall across from the security guard's office. We spent time talking about his life: how he was a great dad, how he was a sensitive and kind person, and how he was successful at many things.

As we discussed the true principles he was learning, I helped him apply them to his situation. He was always quick to produce 'evidence' supporting that these principles just weren't true for his life. Although he believed the principles were true and helpful generally, for every point he would provide evidence how it was not applicable to him.

For instance, as we discussed being open, and bringing integrity into one's life, he said, "Yes, but the fact is that I can't be trusted. I'm just not a trustworthy guy." I would ask him if he wanted to become trustworthy, and he would reply, "Yes, but that's not possible . . ." The yes, but . . . would often include examples of how his wife is justified in not trusting him. He would quickly follow that up with a list of things he had done that prove he was not trustworthy. These reasons were his evidence of why the principles are true, but they just don't apply in his life specifically. To him, he simply could not be trusted, whether he wanted to be trustworthy or not.

With each new principle we would discuss, he would share his "Yes, but . . ." and present his evidence, trying to convince me that the evidence convicted him and he just could not benefit from the otherwise true principle.

How can an otherwise sensitive, kind and caring individual who desires a positive life experience come to the point of believing that absolute truths simply do not apply?

This type of resistance to improvement is often rooted in early failures, which have shaped the person and produced a distorted perception of one's self. It was certainly a stumbling block in this young man's case. In those formative years, a mistake can lead to a thoughtless rebuke, which leads to a self-assigned label, which leads to a lifetime of "yes, but" statements like, "Yes, but, I can never be sober, or trusted, or loved."

I probed for times in this man's life when he had acted in a trustworthy manner. Although he could recite them to me, these examples were the exception to the rule in his mind, not indicative of his true character. If I asked if there was anyone who did trust him, he would say, "Yes, but, that person just doesn't know the real me." In other words, if that person had just known all of the evidence against him, that person would not trust him.

As the weeks and days counted down to his release, I felt a strong desire to at least crack the door and let a tiny bit of light into his understanding that the principles we had been discussing were not only truths for others, but truths for him as well. In a moment of compassion, I felt a strong desire to connect with this man heart to heart.

I looked him squarely in the eyes, and shared from my heart, the greatness I saw in him. I reflected back to him all the intuitive thoughts that had come to me in my weeks of listening to him and hearing his desire beneath the words—he wanted to know he was worthy of love.

As I spoke words of light to him, I saw the light flicker to life in his own eyes. Doubt crept in almost immediately, but there was a moment of trust. He didn't say the words "Yes, but...." Instead, he listened, he heard, and he received.

I know the power of a light received. Once ignited, light is hard to extinguish. I may not be the ultimate recipient of the value he can now give as a result of the value he received in our conversations, but I know that love is being perpetuated somewhere because I walked with him through the Gateway of Charity and was willing to give to him in a way that also paid me. And the beautiful result is that because I was willing to give my whole self away, he was open to receive in a way that paid him. I know that in some way, eventually, I will receive equal or greater value because of the effort I put forth in those hallway conversations —especially the one where I spoke words of light to a man searching for love.

The Transformative Power of Words

Here we begin to see the power of words – the words we speak to ourselves, the words we speak to others, and the words that others speak over us.

Words carry with them the power of life and death. Our attitudes about ourselves and our lives have a tremendous impact on us, and the words we use transform our lives quite literally. Remember my heart attack? I had spoken and journaled the words 'half-hearted attempt' so often that I literally spoke it into existence. The bottom part of my heart physically shut down.

Little did I know the consequences of speaking words over myself. By not confronting the truth, even though I was oblivious to the power within my words, I was creating a new truth for myself, a truth of living a half-hearted life and eventually finding myself in the ER with a half-functioning heart. I had pronounced the sentence of a heart split in two.

What do you think of the power of words now? What self-fulfilling prophecy are you inviting into your future?

We need to guard closely the words we use at all times—when speaking about ourselves, our associates, and especially our children. Children see us as the authority on everything. Words that escape our lips are doctrine to them and are received as truth, regardless of the intent when they were spoken.

Let me relate an experience I had with a woman, whom I will refer to as Barbie. I call her Barbie because she related how she felt her husband looked at her as a Barbie doll—a trophy wife.

When I met with her, she shared her story of health problems, which included a wound that simply appeared one day in the skin of her upper abdomen just below her heart. As of the date I met her, she had endured 22 surgeries and skin grafts attempting to close the wound. The skin grafts often would not 'take.' If the skin graft was successful, the skin around the graft would reject it and it would soon peel off.

This was a very painful and frustrating situation for her. The pain medicine and other medications prescribed to help her condition caused rapid weight gain. Combine that with the open wound and scars from skin grafts and it is understandable to see that her otherwise sexy and attractive body had changed significantly. She painfully revealed to me that her husband spoke harshly to her and physically rejected her because she was no longer the trophy wife, the Barbie doll, he wanted.

Many limiting beliefs about herself were revealed in our first session together that could be summed up in the phrase, "I'm not worthy." It was interesting to find that a memory of her parents seemed to be at the root of this belief. The words that inadvertently came out of her mouth as we delved deeper in this memory told the whole story. Her perception that her parents didn't care about her and that she was powerless to change her circumstances produced words like, "it hurts," "it has left a scar," and predictably, "It's like an open wound that won't heal."

There are really no surprises if we are paying attention. Life brings us exactly what we ask for. All we have to do is speak the hurtful thoughts and emotions that we are hiding inside to know exactly what we are literally creating. In many ways, we get to choose our circumstances. The physical manifestation of our thoughts and beliefs become a huge spotlight on what needs to change.

The universe is literal. I learned this as I looked for the beliefs behind a thickening to the core of my body. Regardless of how I ate or how much I exercised, I just kept feeling heavy in my waist area. On investigation I discovered a belief about not wanting to waste things - food, gifts that others had put personal effort into making by hand, furniture that was still good but I didn't have a place for, the list goes on. Waste...waist, the universe didn't distinguish between the two. I was holding onto things that really should be wasted (thrown in the wastebasket) and my waist was no exception. When I discovered the limiting beliefs that I had to hold onto things that should be wasted, 'miraculously' my digestive system began working properly and it felt all right to let go of waste within my body.

We don't get to choose how the universe brings us what we ask for, but we do get to choose what we ask for. In fact, I encourage you to try it for yourself. Right now, pick an experience that happened recently...even today...where you were annoyed or upset by what someone else did or said. Focus on it and identify what your overwhelming thought was about that person or about you in that moment. Does the statement start with he should... or I should... or something else as equally judgmental? That is perfect! Follow the steps to your Permission Process! When you have crafted some new beliefs that allow you to create a different outcome, post them somewhere you can read them often. Put all your faith into these new beliefs and consciously look for evidence that they are already true. Then watch as your experience completely transforms. Remember, the universe will bring your outcome in one of three ways:

1. The universe may bring you a different outcome in the form of the person being removed from our life. Perhaps they get transferred to a different department at work or they move to a different state.
2. The universe may bring you a different outcome in the form of the person changing how they act, to align with what you now believe about them or yourself. Perhaps they attend a seminar on unconditional love and begin seeing you as a compassionate person who is only trying to help, and in the process they express more gratitude.
3. The Universe may bring you a different outcome in the form of the person staying completely the same, but it doesn't bother you anymore. Perhaps you begin to see that only you are bothered by the dirty dishes and you decide that you really like to keep the kitchen clean yourself, so you don't expect them to do it anymore.

Evidence that Facilitates Freedom

Often, people tend to put too much value on past experiences. Although it is true that we learn from the past, especially our own past experiences, we still frequently wake up each morning enslaved by what happened yesterday. If we are not willing to begin anew each day, our yesterdays will imprison our present.

Some clients tell me about their past mistakes, sometimes from decades earlier, and they explain that those mistakes are why today went poorly. They tell me about a problem they had last year, and tell me that is why they are disqualified from taking any of the leaps of faith they desire, and why they are prohibited from living at any level of happiness and fulfillment.

On the other hand, other clients surround themselves with trophies they won last year or 20 years ago and tell me that this was the pinnacle of their lives. They hold onto this success and let it block further progress. Just like those with mistakes, those who are clinging to past successes are also unable to move forward and become more. They are likewise being enslaved by the past, unable to fully live in the present moment.

What I do with both groups of people is ask them to broaden the evidence they see, to stop being so selective in presenting their evidence. At least stop cherry picking evidence from the past that proves they don't measure up. It doesn't really matter what happened yesterday anyway, because today is a new day. Each day starts with a new beginning, a new dawn.

Dawn. What a wonderful, predictable space in time. Have you ever made a trek to a special place in the dark so that you could witness the dawn deliberately? What is the enticement for having this type of experience?

A turning point for me comes to mind with this question. I had a life-altering decision to make. I chose a favorite lakefront cabin for my place of meditation. I arose before the sun and dressed in a soft, cozy pullover sweater, warming me against the late September weather. The morning was silent as all other beach-goers had already locked up after the final summer fling in preparation for colder temperatures. The lake was all but abandoned by everyone. Only the wildlife remained.

I went to the shed to select a lightweight, comfy chair in preparation for an extensive connective moment with nature. I walked the quarter mile or so of beach before finally arriving at the water's edge. There was no breeze this particular morning. As I tiptoed through a shallow pool and selected the perfect sandbar to set up my chair, I felt tremendous gratitude for the silence.

The water was a mirror of the sky, liquid glass. As the light gently stretched forth on the distance horizon, I was struck by my inability to distinguish the water from the sky. Both were still, the perfect reflection of color. Emotion overwhelmed me and my pen flew across the page as I poured out my heart on paper.

What began as long-hand script, became bullet points of ideas, pros and cons, random thoughts that were somehow connected. With no judgment of how it should look or where the destination lay, I continued to write. In the distant trees behind me, I heard birds begin to bust forth in song and then...I watched the sun break between sky and sea. And then came a simultaneous brightness of understanding. The clarity of my impending choice was as definitive as the horizon now before me. Where before there had been indistinguishable lines, the same shade of blue from my feet to eternity, I now saw the outline of small ripples in shimmering water.

Dawn. The beginning of all possibilities. The first words of creation were "let there be light." The welcome light of morning after a distressing night of darkness—figuratively and literally—this is dawn. The quiet, calm light that brings a peace that defies all chaos sometimes present in darkness, a new beginning—this is dawn. A leap of faith taken in a new direction can sometimes feel like leaping into the dark, but I submit that the opposite is actually true. When we take that first step into the unknown, we are truly leaping from the dark into the earliest light of dawn, defying the darkness, reaching towards a new beginning.

A practice that has served me is to pour out my heart every night in gratitude and let the Lord fill my heart up every morning, with inspired next steps. If we can learn to do that, to hit the reset button every night and then to start life over every morning, just as God does with the new dawn, then we can begin to understand that today does not need to be influenced negatively by yesterday or last year.

Looking to the past does have its place, but we need to be selective in how we let the past influence us. It serves us to look backwards to find evidence of the good, to find proof that we do measure up. It also serves to look backwards to find the root of a limiting belief when we have the intention of changing it. The past holds evidence that we are worthy of great things in our lives.

After a breakthrough, I ask clients to focus on the positive evidences in their lives that prove the new belief is actually more true than the old limiting belief they were holding onto. Frequently my clients are able to find strong reminders of the truth of their good choices in no time at all. When examined in the light of dawn, those evidences are more true than the negative ones they had more readily believed just moments before. The past holds evidence of all truth. We just have to look for evidence of the truth, not the lies from our limiting beliefs.

My parolee student from my earlier example, was able to look deeply in his heart and find overwhelming evidence of his trustworthiness. He, who was so quick to marshal evidence of his untrustworthy nature, when prompted, began seeing himself in that new light of trust. He looked to the past to find proof of a new, more empowering belief, and he made a commitment to become that trustworthy person.

The practice of seeking evidence can be helpful in finding courage to leap to each new level. For instance, a person who is having trouble letting go of past experiences of procrastination or sabotaging his success, can visualize the dawn of a new way of being. A farmer goes to all of the trouble of preparing his soil, fertilizing, and planting seeds, watering, and weeding without knowing for sure that his crops will grow, or that he will be able to harvest them several months later. After all of his work and investment, he doesn't know for sure that he will be able to sell his crops for money to support his family. Crops often fail. Many times, nature creates an interrupt in the crop-growing process that creates an impossibility for success.

Why then does a farmer go to all of that trouble and expense, if he knows there is no guarantee that his crops will succeed? We could ask the same question about any business person. Businesses fail, yet millions of people start up new businesses every year. They invest their money, their reputation, their security, and their time. Why would they do that if there's a chance they will fail?

The question can be answered in one word: belief.

When we interrupt our pattern of thought long enough to notice all of the evidence in their lives that we are smart, trustworthy, industrious, honest, thrifty, wise, etc., we have an easier time envisioning ourselves as the person we wish to become and the life we wish to live. When the way we are living presently is no longer enough, as faith-filled beings, we begin to formulate a vision of what's next. We envision what it will take to get to that next level. Each new level is a new dawn—a welcome light, a peace and calm, a beginning of all possibilities. The next gateway, the Gateway of Prosperity will help you understand when it is time to move from one level to the next.

When I'm mentoring someone who resists seeing the evidence of his abilities, and instead focuses on evidence that he can't accomplish something, I ask him to question his evidence:

Questions like, "Is that absolutely true? Is that a universal truth? Does it apply to every person on the planet?" These questions help him to look at facts rather than false beliefs. He'll then tell me about people and instances where it hasn't been that way.

I think, "Yes! A chink in the armor of a long-standing and strong, yet untrue belief!"

"Well, then," I'll say, "It's not an absolute truth. It's just something that you've chosen to believe. It's not a truth but a belief, and by the evidence of the examples you just gave me, it's a false belief."

Then I'll take the opportunity to expound on the evidence proving the new, somewhat foreign, yet true principle. We can add to the truth of the new belief by checking to see if this has been useful to others. The more he expands his understanding that the principle actually works, at least for others who have used it, the more he is open to find evidence in his own life as well.

I teach my clients to seek evidence that the opposite of their limiting belief is not only true, but that it can teach them that what they really wish they could believe is true right now. Let me give you an example. If the belief is "I can't trust myself." I ask him if he can trust himself to eat when he is hungry, bathe when he is stinky, put the right shoe on the right foot, etc. If he can trust himself in the most minute way, he can honestly say, "I trust me," and believe it!

As soon as he can believe something new, he liberates himself to begin creating something new. He is no longer enslaved by experiences of the past, which he has allowed to keep himself from moving forward. New possibilities and opportunities begin to open for him, and he begins to lay a new foundation by envisioning his next level of serving in his own unique way.

What is Truth?

As we're talking about belief and truth, it's important to recognize that the only thing there is that is worth believing in or trusting is truth. Yet in today's world, the simple concept of truth has become clouded with confusing half-truths and misconceptions. So before we go on, I want you to fully understand the simple yet profound truth about 'truth.'

I have talked a lot about beliefs, my truths (or your truths), and the highest truth. Let's make sure we understand these definitions for each of these. What's the difference between a belief and a truth? If someone believes something, it is true for that person because they have decided it is true. To reach our full potential we must seek and align with the highest truths which are the truths that we all agree are true. An example of highest truth is gravity pulling objects towards the earth.

So if someone is operating under their truth—a belief that is being honored as an absolute but isn't really because it applies only to them—and if it is really not serving them to believe it, then I sometimes ask, "Is that absolutely true for everyone?" If the answer is no, it isn't absolutely true for everyone, then they can see that their truth is merely a belief (usually a limiting belief). As such, they can choose a new belief. They may choose to keep the limiting belief but now they know it is a conscious choice to keep believing and not a situation they have no control over.

Here's an example of one of my old limiting beliefs. While on a certain business trip the thought came to me, "The second night in a hotel while I'm traveling, I never sleep quite as well." In that moment, I heard myself think the belief, and I immediately chose to challenge the thought. I stopped and asked myself if my statement was absolutely true for everyone. Of course it wasn't. Many people stay in hotels and sleep soundly the second night of their stay.

I asked myself, "Do I want that to be true for me?" The answer was, "Of course not." I wanted to get a good night's sleep on night number two as well. Based on my response, I chalked it up as a mere belief. Even though I had formerly accepted it as a truth, putting it to the test now, and exposing it to the light of universality, I realized that it was not true. And guess what? The outcome of my new belief, "I sleep soundly wherever I am" was that my second night was as peaceful and restful as the first.

Here is another truth that I had adopted: "Brushing my teeth after I eat is a good habit." As I inspected it and tested it against the standard of universality, I decided that it is true for just about everyone. Because it works for me as well, I chose to accept it as one of my truths that is close to a universal truth even though it may not be true for everyone.

I know there are some who will not accept this belief as an absolute truth for them, so I am not planning to teach this in one of my book. But if someone asked me about good hygiene practices, I would probably share this as something that is my truth. Once I accept the truth of it, I don't have to make another decision about it when I eat next time. It's already been accepted as truth, so my body and mind honor it. It feels weird if I don't follow through once it is an accepted truth.

Our bodies and minds level up with our belief systems. When we accept something as truth, good or not so good, we naturally align with it. It feels weird if we do something that goes against any of our beliefs. We want to be in integrity. That is the science behind choosing a new belief and having evidence naturally start showing up to support the new belief.

The end result of these changes is living a life constantly aligned with highest truth we currently understand. Every change starts with choosing to have a different outcome. Then we choose a new belief that allows us to experience this new outcome, then we see evidences proving our belief as truth. When we fully adopt the new belief as truth, we don't have to make daily decisions or read daily affirmations anymore—it just is.

Love Creates Synergy

Most people achieve a certain level of success on their own, without having ever heard about the Seven Gateways and without mentoring. They rise to what they feel is expected of them or what they expect of themselves. If they are less ambitious than that, then they rise to what they think is acceptable in our society or their family unit.

A few people find a way to grow simply out of love for themselves. Without an earth-bound mentor to talk with and receive feedback from, and without the synergy of working with others around them, the process can be tedious, long, and wrought with painful cycles and lessons. That's why the Gateway of Charity is so crucial. When we work together in our gifted capacity, the creation period is shortened and the impact is broadened.

Let me explain how I have embodied the Gateway of Charity as a final summary to this chapter.

I invite people to show up—to be their full, authentic, best, true selves. I give to them all that I have and all that I am, and I invite them to do the same. More than invite, I anticipate, or even expect it from them. Expecting integrity of character and action is the greatest gift I can give them. Anything less or more would not be in alignment.

This invitation to be a certain way is only offered because I see who they are. And I know they can see me as clearly as I can see them. Even if I am trying to hide something, I will be seen because we are mirrors for each other. Therefore, there are no secrets. I'm showing up in full clarity and so are you. You and I are communicating heart to heart, soul to soul, whether we know it or not.

My friend who was on parole thought he was hiding. In reality there are no masks. If I invite you to partner with me in my creation, it is because of who you are, whether you are consistently living or being that or not. There is no pretending to try to do our 'best.' Energetic bonds are formed with each other based on what we know about the gifts we each possess. An energetic contract has fine print that reads, "show me who you are, show me the best you—the best you can be. And I will do the same."

This invitation we extend gives others permission to become

who they really want to be. My intention and desire, is to see you for who you truly are—whether you have realized your potential yet or not. I seek to see the highest and best form of you and invite you to be that person. I invite you by letting you see that version of you reflected in my eyes. This process creates a safe place to try your wings in a way you may have never dared or trusted before.

I visited Machu Picchu in Peru recently and was inspired by the obvious synergy that was present in the city's glory days. Everything pointed to leaders and community members alike utilizing the Gateway of Charity to establish the most successful civilization for every citizen. There was an appointment made for each person in how they served. Their appointment was based in interests, talents and what benefited the community best.

In the early days of America, there was a similar system. Each young man when he came of age, selected a profession to study based on talents and interests. He even worked for free to attain a trade or profession that served the community. Likewise, the Gateway of Charity invites you to serve in a way that serves you, and to invite others to serve you in a way that serves them.

Your Rite of Passage through the Gateway of Charity
How Aligned Are You with Charity?

Evaluate yourself on a scale of 1-5 (5 is completely aligned):
1. I am willing to give my best to benefit others in a way that serves them and me equally. I expect equal value for the value I give. I leverage the genius of others to exponentially magnify my creation and to give them an opportunity to utilize their unique gifts. I am able to embrace many more opportunities because I am surrounded by talented people who are benefited by participating in my creations. I give my best and anticipate that others will do the same.
2. I step out of judgment and see others in their greatness. I invite them to show up that way, fully expecting that they are capable of it. I speak of them and to them as if I am speaking directly to the purest form of them. I am conscious of my purest form as well and expect to be respected and honored in a way that aligns with my standard.
3. I recognize my greatness and the unique way that I serve. There is no competition because only I serve people in my genius way. I offer myself freely with no fear that others might rise above me. We are each acting within our special gifts and we need each other to reach the highest point in the fastest time and with the most powerful result.
4. I am aware of the transformative power of words. I am conscious of the words I speak to others. I only speak words that give life and growth, never words that are destructive or demeaning. I create with my words. I love myself so much that I only choose powerful, positive and uplifting words for myself and others. I speak the greatness I see in others. I acknowledge the greatness I see in myself.

The Seven Gateways

The Seven Gateways

THE FOURTH GATEWAY- PROSPERITY

The Counterfeit

I believed in a false success that I was building on my terms. I thought I could create prosperity in my little corner and no one would notice. I felt like a change-maker making a difference. However, I was out of alignment with the bigger creation that I was part of. In that work setting, I was not allowed to be me because my values didn't match the bigger vision of a controlling employer who saw everyone else as beneath him. I saw greatness in others, he saw disappointment and unimportance. He did not have charity. He could not see the potential within others as Christ does.

The Truth

True success and prosperity is achieved when there is a common goal or cause, and the perfect people from the Gateway of Charity who are in alignment with that goal or cause, are invited to be part of it. Ironically, success in a negative environment can be achieved when all are seeking the same outcome. However, the Gateway of Prosperity is reserved for those that exhibit charity by inviting all who choose to participate, to give their all for their own positive benefit as well as for the benefit of the team. Anyone can achieve a level of monetary success. But for it to be authentic prosperity, they must first pass through the Gateway of Charity.

Again, notice that the work that was required in the first gateway of the pair (Charity), gives us a new level of synthesizing information and integrating it to be able to recognize the truth within the following gateway (Prosperity). Internalizing charity gives a new layer of depth that seeps into the heart and creates a spiritual, emotional and physical bond between people that is necessary for genuine lasting prosperity.

My Assessment

For me, authentic prosperity is not possible where charity does not exist. I am not creating authentic success because those in charge of the bigger picture are not in alignment with my methods of working with people. The counterfeit is that I can be prosperous in any environment by being me, giving my best and sincerely believing that I am making a difference. I think it's just a mindset. I can will it to be.

The truth is that I can only be truly prosperous where I am giving my best to a creation that is in alignment with me.

Because I have not learned how the Gateway of Charity leads to the Gateway of Prosperity, I can't figure out why my efforts constantly backfire. When I don't know about the truth vs the counterfeit in this situation, it becomes an inner game. I make the decision that I AM a disappointment, rather than my choice, my boss, my job is a disappointment. It is not my circumstances that are bad, it is me that is bad. Living in the counterfeit skews my view. I cannot receive a genuine outcome when I am putting effort toward a counterfeit belief.

Entering The Gateway of Prosperity

Understanding the truth of charity leads to genuine prosperity (the next gateway). In business, it is extremely important to grasp the truth of the Gateway of Charity. Author Walter Isaacson of the book Steve Jobs quotes Jobs as saying, "When you have really good people, you don't have to baby them. By expecting them to do great things, you can get them to do great things. A-plus players like to work together, and they don't like it if you tolerate B-grade work."

Steve Jobs had charity. He looked within individuals for their talents, and expected them to perform within their genius at the same level that he demanded of himself within his genius. Jobs also said, "It doesn't make sense to hire smart people and tell them what to do; we hire smart people so they can tell us what to do."

Steve Jobs understood the value of finding individuals who resonated with the culture of his business, and were gifted in a way that supported what he was creating. He allowed them to free flow within their genius, and the result was exponential prosperity.

If you have been taking action as you have been reading, then you have successfully navigated three gateways on your way to a happy and fulfilling life. A happy and fulfilling life is where who you are and what you are creating is in alignment. You have probably experienced faith several times. Each time, you have likely discovered that when you step out in faith, abundance awaits you outside your comfort zone. You have begun to see resources and information where you once only saw chaos. Then you have gathered those resources, some in the form of people with skills you need, and you have utilized charity to leverage their skills to your benefit. With all of these tools and knowledge in hand, I can only imagine the peace and prosperity you are now noticing in your life! I am guessing that you also have begun manifesting the life of your dreams.

"When you arrive at a place where faith, abundance, and charity exist together, you let go of the need to control. Since you don't need to control anything, the universe is free to work on manifesting your dreams without your interference. That is the moment you've arrived at the Gateway of Prosperity."

The Gateway of Prosperity is a place in time. The moment you recognize the success that you have already manifested, you feel gratitude for it. You could even say that you have 'arrived.' Even if you have not realized the full measure of your original vision, you most definitely can see how you have changed and become more prepared to receive what you are hoping to manifest in the near future.

Sometimes our vision has actually become a reality and we just don't see it. We get so focused on the path to get there and the habits that create it that we miss the celebration!

As you work towards your Gateway of Prosperity, I would like to have you practice four steps:
1. Check in daily to see how prosperity is already manifesting in your life.
2. Express gratitude for every small evidence that proves you are already there.
3. Continue to ask how your goal can be perfected and even more complete.
4. Celebrate any milestone achieved, no matter how small.

I remember when the Gateway of Prosperity happened upon me for a particular goal. It dawned on me as I focusing on my vision board. I had been so focused on how the end result should look that I didn't realize my goal had already been achieved! When I really opened myself to see how my goal may already be a reality, I saw that it was actually done! As we have already learned, we put an order in to the universe by the words we write and speak. The way I had written my intention had been manifested perfectly. I think it will help you see what I mean if I share exactly what happened.

A couple of years ago, I had an audacious dream to have a beach house, a mountain cabin, and an artist's retreat in a desert community. I knew at the time it was far-fetched—I didn't have the money for such nonsense. But I had a very strong reason behind this desire and I was willing to risk failure to get it. A goal, no matter how far-fetched, is worthy and righteous when the reason behind it supports your purpose.

Many of my clients and friends who follow my work know that

I have a desire to hold retreats in various settings to help people interrupt their destructive everyday cycles and reconnect with themselves, those they love, and God. I have held several of these retreats in different locations within three hours of my home. Each time, I rented a home to create a family feeling, and to get away from society and the beliefs that are prevalent there. I like to create a fully immersive experience.

I am limited on the number of people I can serve hosting my events this way. Also, there are only so many retreats I can create in a year without a staff to support me. I am tremendously grateful for how I have been able to serve in my current capacity, but I also know there is a higher and more impactful way I can serve. One of these ways is hosting my retreats in various locations around the United States with a full staff.

After a couple of years, as you may imagine, my goal seemed so far away that one day I took it down off the wall. Even as I write this, I feel the heaviness in my heart that accompanied the decision that the time for this goal was just not now. I disobeyed one of the key rules of manifesting! I doubted. I didn't throw the pictures or the goal away; I knew that someday in the future this might possibly be a reality. I did doubt though. I made the decision that having a mountain home, a beach home, and an artist retreat in the desert was not for me at that time.

Then came the miracle.

Soon after removing this goal from my vision board I attended a family event. While there, one of my relatives reminded me that they have invited us to their desert home—complete with a private casita—several times, and we had never taken them up on it. My husband and I committed to visit by scheduling a 3-day retreat with them.

I awoke the next morning with a vision of what had been manifested—I had a desert home! And then I saw clearly in my mind how all of my requests had already been granted. I have a friend in southern California who lives about 10 minutes from the beach. She has a guest house and has invited me to come and stay with her at any time. Bam! My beach house was a reality! I have another friend who just moved to the east coast and has invited me to visit any time. She has a home with separate guest quarters not far from the beach. Bam! Another beach house in another location across the country! I live in the Rocky Mountain area and we have awesome mountain views and a great backyard filled with aspens and pines. In less than 5 minutes I can be hiking up my favorite mountain trail and taking in all the joys and beauties of nature. Bam! My mountain home was already in existence.

I ran to the file where I had stashed my dream and quickly slapped it back up on my vision board. Everything I had written had come into existence! And not only that, it had been mine for over a year–I just didn't notice.

This vision really anchored in lessons I had learned before, but until that moment, I didn't have the physical evidence for the lessons to become part of who I was. Until this realization hit me, I had forgotten that faith is required until the imagined result becomes real. After this experience, doubting became harder and faith became easier.

So is this the end of the retreat manifesting story? Hardly! As I write this section, I am sitting in my relative's beautiful desert home with a mountain view outside the dining room window. It is perfect, and it isn't enough. What I have is awesome! I am grateful and content with the access that I have to these beautiful retreat locations...for me. But I know that there is more. I know that I can serve at an even higher level when I have a larger space that is mine to schedule as it is time to hold a retreat.

So those homes are still on my vision board and I have added more words to bring this into reality faster: "My retreat locations enable me to teach and inspire those who are seeking to ascend to higher levels of integrity and freedom. I am open to the perfect locations becoming accessible for me, for my family, and for those I serve." I already know this is actually on the way because I have another friend who is building a mountain cabin and has already told me I can hold my retreats there when it is complete.

This experience taught me so many things. First, I learned that when I put in my order, it is on its way. I also learned that it is super important to word my creation exactly the way I want it to look when it arrives, but I recognize the importance of being open for the universe to bring my order to me in whatever way is best for me in my state of preparation. Apparently I am only ready and prepared to receive the retreats so that my family and I can enjoy them. There must be some lessons I still need to learn before I can have full access to a large retreat location for others to enjoy. While I am waiting, I prepare myself for the inevitable. I become the person I need to be to receive this gift from the universe.

I learned further that there is almost always a way in the present moment for me to believe that what I am asking for already exists. Rather than just rattling off my affirmations and looking at the pictures with unseeing eyes, I have deliberately opened myself to believe and imagine that it is already a reality. This makes it easy to state my visions and goals in the present tense as if they already exist...because they do! And since they already exist, when I say I have a resort in a desert, a mountain, and a beach location, it feels true and it is true! Even the universe has to believe me because I believe it myself. The final lesson I learned is to never doubt. Always be ready to receive. Always have full faith that your goal is on its way, and be sure to notice when it shows up.

Noticing when our goal shows up—even in the smallest of ways—is very important. When we recognize all the ways we have already been blessed with our goal or vision, we shorten the gestation period.

With the goal of having retreat locations around the nation, I have been able to shorten the gestation time of receiving what I choose because I have allowed myself to see how it has been brought to me almost immediately in some small way. I am manifesting more easily and quickly than ever by doing this one thing: shifting my mind to see that what I want is already in my possession in some way.

My idea of what my goal looked like is a little different than what it actually was. But the essence of what I was seeking was perfect. I had manifested a place of comfort and peace—a sanctuary that is separate from the daily cycles where we get stuck. This is a milestone. It is evidence that what I see in my imagination is on the way, I am just not quite at the finish line.

The Multiplying Effect of Gratitude

Before I walked through the Gateway of Charity on my way to the Gateway of Prosperity, my journey was somewhat self-centered. I am grateful that I have learned how much others benefit when I use charity to invite them to get behind my cause.

We've heard that the lifeguard is the strongest swimmer at the beach. I appreciate the truth of that axiom. It helps us understand that in order to be in a position to help others achieve what they desire, we have to pull ourselves out of the mire. We have to have already become proficient, perhaps having even mastered a skill, before we can teach others. This means we have to focus on our own Gateway of Prosperity before we can guide someone else through it.

It seemed selfish to me that I would put so much focus on my own end result, but I realize how unselfish it truly is. I am giving my life to gather the wisdom to share with others who may not find the way without help. Wisdom only comes through applied knowledge from personal experience.

This leads us to the importance of gratitude. All creation begins and ends with gratitude. The Gateway of Prosperity beckons us to take stock regularly of everything good that we have in our lives. This includes possessions, people, love, opportunities, and even obstacles. The act of counting our blessings, even if a blessing looks like a curse, works in any circumstance. It is the key to attracting what we want.

We usually think of gratitude as being thankful for someone or something that we love or that gives us joy. But there are certain circumstances that are not considered joyful by most people. What then?

It is perfectly appropriate to have negative feelings about certain circumstances. It is normal. But what if I told you that finding gratitude in that circumstance, stops its creation? How quickly could you find gratitude for your situation? Believe it or not, you can feel negative emotions about an experience and be grateful for it at the same time. When I was teaching a weekly class for the local county jail, I asked how many in the class were grateful they had been sent to jail. Over half of the hands went up.

The law of attraction dictates that we attract what we focus on. So if we focus on something that we don't want, it comes to us just as fast as something we focus on that we do want. Focusing on the good in a bad situation and feeling gratitude for it brings you more good things you can be grateful for. Negative feelings are certainly okay initially, but feeling gratitude eliminates the need for perpetual negative feelings about our circumstances.

Another aspect of the law of attraction teaches that stating what we want in the present tense, as if it already exists, is required for successfully attracting new results. For example, let's say you have a husband who is super tight with money. There is plenty of money but he questions everything you spend it on. You feel very angry at him about the money you finally get to spend. It escalates to the point that you wish you had your own money so you could spend it however you want. So much energy goes into that anger that your husband loses his job and you have to go to work to support the family. Now you have your own money; you're the sole money-maker.

That is Law of Attraction 101 – you focused on having your own money to spend and now all the money coming in is yours. However, your husband lost his job in the process. How can you find gratitude in that?

Let's take the same scenario and insert gratitude. Your husband is super tight with money. There is plenty of it, but he questions everything you spend it on. You tell all your friends how grateful you are that your husband is such a good steward over money and feels responsibility for every penny he brings into the home. You ask and receive with gratitude the money he offers. Additionally, you receive with gratitude the mentoring he offers about the value of investments. You never have to work a day in your life because your husband is so good at taking care of all the financial details.

I know these are absolute scenarios and no circumstance is a perfect example. However, using this example, can you see how a little piece of gratitude might be feeling grateful that you have money to feel angry about? Another source of gratitude could be noticing why the thing that bugs you (husband asks about every penny) is actually a source of gratitude (husband is a great steward of money). Pure gratitude inspires us to love the circumstance rather than trying to find gratitude even though we feel anger.

In the above example, the wife chose into gratitude about the way her husband handles money—the very thing she was angry about in the first place! Is that kind of gratitude hard? It can be. But it is also simple—as simple as choosing to find and feel gratitude.

What have you been seeing as a thorn in your side that is actually a gift? If you can find one tiny bit of gratitude, it opens the door for a bad situation to become good. In our previous example, I could just as easily say, "my husband is a good provider" as I could say, "my husband is a tightwad." It is my choice. One choice leads to a feeling of financial security, the other leads to a feeling of financial scarcity. If I want a financially secure life with freedom when it comes to money, and I don't want to go to work myself, which decision opens the door to what I want the fastest? Find the gratitude and you get what you want; find the pain and you get what you don't want.

The trick about gratitude is that when you find it, you no longer need to learn the lessons of that circumstance. You can circumvent problems by finding gratitude in any and all situations, especially ones that are difficult and less than ideal. Try it!

Gratitude is realizing that everything is a gift. It is acknowledging our total reliance on power outside of, and often greater, than ourselves. The plentitude of the universe is available to us, and we are free to harvest and shape it into anything we desire. Wow! Do you see how abundant and free we are to create? Gratitude is a key factor if we are to continue having access to this abundance and freedom.

If abundance is so plentiful, then why do we hear of poverty in America, with many Americans living at or below the poverty level? Why is this true in a country with so much opportunity, abundance and prosperity? Some will say that we haven't done enough spending of our collective resources on the impoverished to help them out of their circumstances—that we should "redistribute the wealth." However, according to The Heritage Foundation, America has actually spent over $20 trillion in the past 50 years to eradicate poverty, completely failing in the process. In fact, it seems that poverty expands exponentially for every dollar we spend to eliminate it. How can this be?

It is because poverty is a mindset of not finding gratitude in what one has.

I have traveled outside America where the most affluent people would be considered poor by our standards. Yet they don't know they are poor. They have not adopted the beliefs of poverty. They are grateful and happy. In fact, while recently in Peru, I was struck by the absolute creativity the mountain people had in using all the resources around them to create a rainbow of colors for their beautifully dyed textiles. Even adding a gemstone to water with flowers, created a different color! These people were poor by our standards, but they were rich in gratitude. Therefore, they lived happy, productive, prosperous lives. I actually had the thought while watching the women dying their llama wool, "Look how rich they are! They have everything!"

Every now and then we read the stories of those who somehow catch the vision, and determine to step out in faith, find abundance, invite charity, and finally land in prosperity, regardless of their circumstances. Sonya Carson comes to mind when I think of such people. She was a woman who struggled in poverty and was plagued with mental illness. She refused to see the world from that viewpoint, however, and despite her surroundings, she created opportunities for herself and her children. In the midst of her struggles she imprinted on her children a sense of abundance and prosperity and helped them take the leap from where they were to the next level, then the next and the next. Many years later one of her sons, Dr. Ben Carson, is a world-renowned brain surgeon, presidential candidate, and as of this writing, the nation's Secretary of the Department of Housing and Urban Development. His mother inspired him to think beyond his circumstances, and now he resides in prosperity and continues to bless lives through his talents and skills. I can only imagine the gratitude he has for his mother as a mentor in his early years.

Gratitude is powerful. Every word in the English language has a vibration of energy. Lower vibration words are fear-based words like worry and anger. Love-based words like joy and happiness have higher vibrations. The energy and vibration of the word gratitude is proven to be one of the highest vibration words we are aware of. When we live in gratitude we live at a higher vibration and energy. Remember, energy attracts like energy. If I am speaking and feeling gratitude, then I am inviting more high vibration experiences into my life.

I feel so certain that inviting gratitude into our daily lives empowers us to create more of what we want in our lives that I do a Daily Gratitude Call https://wylenebenson.com/gratitude/#gratitude every morning with all of my clients who choose to join me. The call is also a podcast available on all the major podcast platforms. There are so many things to be grateful for: clean running water from the faucet, endless supplies of inexpensive, tasty foods regardless of the season, a day's wages to jump on a plane to fly a thousand miles in two hours, instant communication with friends and family around the world, an on-call doctor in case we have an emergency, freedom to do almost anything we desire. The list is truly endless.

The Gateway of Prosperity is built upon gratitude for what we have in the present moment. It is a celebration space where we can enjoy what we have created and have fun with our well-deserved results for a time. There is great abundance and opportunity all around us. So much is made available to us from the efforts of others and from the abundance of the earth.

Prosperity Extends Beyond Ourselves

Gratitude for all our gifts, blessings, and overwhelming prosperity turns our hearts to blessing and serving others. This is why it is so important, vital even, to reach and live in prosperity. When we see all we have, we notice that we have enough and more—plenty to give and serve those around us. Arriving at this realization that there is enough and to spare, prepares us for the upcoming Gateway of Obedience. You will learn why in the next chapter.

I have heard some say they don't want to make a lot of money. They only want enough for their needs. Initially this sounds like a humble goal. While having enough for their needs is great for them, it's not so great for the rest of humanity. If we stop at serving ourselves, we become reliant on only what we can produce individually. We are each self-serving. If everything we do is just for ourselves, most of us will find it tedious to always have to go it alone, and at some point will lose the will to grow. Rather than being content with what we have, we become complacent with mediocrity.

We are not made to serve only ourselves, but to lift and serve those around us. Think of the Gateway of Charity and how no one person can—or should—do everything alone. We need each other.

Altruism and philanthropy are an essential part of a thriving society. If we can produce beyond our needs, we can become part of the flow of abundance for the greater good and help others with their dreams as well. Our example of gratitude in prosperity may be just the inspiration another needs to take their first leap of faith to build a better life for themselves. Or perhaps the little extra we have created beyond our own needs can help provide a stable foundation for someone who has not quite reached the Gateway of Prosperity for themselves.

Enjoying prosperity can be just for you, or it can be extended to family, friends, communities, and even the world, perpetuating the flow and cycle of abundance. Prosperity alone, is lonely. Experiencing it with those who helped you create it is fulfilling. We are all one. We all want the same things.

In your place of prosperity, you may share your abundance with others by volunteering for worthy causes, serving in your church or service organization, or involving yourself politically. Prosperity could be a draw toward world travel to do humanitarian work or opening a daycare in your home to give kids a place they can feel love and acceptance outside of family. Regardless of your dream, there will be a moment in prosperity when you feel yourself desiring to reach out to others. The perfect way for you to bless and serve will hit your awareness and you'll step into a higher place of giving than ever before along your journey. Remember, the Gateway of Abundance taught you that if the reason behind your service allows you to receive at the same time you are serving —whether monetarily or emotionally – it will perpetuate the flow of abundance and you will always be filled.

There are so many successful people around the world who live in this place of prosperity and bless so many lives. I know a retired businessman who offers a mentoring program for disadvantaged students at a major university. He provides them with everything they need to get into college, study effectively, and make the right contacts in school and afterward. He has seen hundreds of youth from poorer neighborhoods graduate from college then begin great careers or start successful companies.

Another business executive heads up the financial responsibilities of The Wounded Warrior Project, something he is extremely passionate about and a cause that blesses numerous lives

I have a friend and mentor—a billionaire—who anonymously donates millions of dollars every year for the benefit of his employees, community, and even strangers he feels inspired to bless. His gift is making money, and he has stepped beyond his own personal Gateway of Prosperity to help others in their journey in the way he knows best.

I know of a married couple who not only donates money, but they also travel to Haiti and the Dominican Republic to build schools and playgrounds for disadvantaged children. They also donate huge amounts to international relief efforts for disasters all over the world.

Another friend plans trips to Africa and gives 100% of the donations she collects to build schools and water systems for the communities there. Those who work with her pay their own way and donate time and supplies.

Many others, who are not necessarily wealthy, offer their gift to the world in their unique ways. Some run blogs, providing free research and useful or fun information for millions of people to use as they wish. Others write books and give them away online. Still more serve in their communities, giving of their time, talents, and money in ways that bless others and fulfill them. There is an increased level of service and giving when someone resides in Prosperity and feels gratitude for all they've been given.

What's Holding You Back?

In a way, it was easier to envision my first leap of faith than it was to envision walking through the Gateway of Prosperity. In those early innocent days of discovering my path of purpose, I was blissfully ignorant to what was really going to be required to reach my goal. After days and weeks of focused action—breaking through my limiting beliefs as they came up, gathering people, learning skills, doing the uncomfortable—I finally reached the threshold of the Gateway of Prosperity. I knew I was close to achieving a new level of influence, and honestly, it frightened me. The fear of success and the resulting spotlight was something I was not ready for.

Working with a mentor, in an attempt to embrace the next inevitable level, I allowed myself to see in my mind's eye, the reality of the fear I was feeling. In this visualization, I saw a strap tied around my ankle. I saw myself standing on a mountaintop, above the clouds, on the edge of a bottomless abyss. I intuitively knew that what I wanted was across the expanse. I could see my landing point clearly, and yet I was tethered to the ground by the strap around my ankle. Even if I had been able to move, working up the courage to jump from the edge, the very real fear of missing my mark and free-falling kept me rooted where I stood.

Still, I felt the overwhelming desire to try. In my imagination, I fashioned a hatchet to chop through the strap. I worked desperately, but it was as if I were chopping through iron. It was impossible to free myself.

As I struggled to break the strap that held me bound, a new thought came to me. The hatchet disappeared and I calmly, deliberately bent down and simply untied the tether.

I had the power to release myself all along. It was my own

fear that was holding me bound. Once I was free of that fear, I instantaneously took courage. I, as myself, still didn't know if I was capable of landing safely across the deep and wide chasm before me. So I called upon my higher self. I asked the question: "who would I be if I were fully committed?"

I was mesmerized as I watched myself transform into a sleek and powerful warrior with the keen instinct and courage of a majestic jungle cat. Without my conscious prompting, this beautiful creature took three giant steps backwards, then bolted forward and leapt from the edge. I literally felt physical wings unfold from my back and carry me easily to my destination.

What holds you back from leaping across the void that separates you from your Gateway of Prosperity? What does the tether around your ankle (the reason why you can't) represent to you?

Of course, our obstacles are imaginary, but we are greatly influenced by what we imagine to be true. Until we find the courage to jump, we will never feel our wings.

When you have become the person who aligns with what you are seeking, it is just a matter of time before it becomes a physical reality.

Since overcoming that fear, I continue to lead and place myself in the spotlight in order to share what I believe is my purpose—and I have found myself in the line of fire from those who are not on the same path as me. I have also found that I am given the words, the support and the skills to rise above it. Can you trust that you are enough? Can you trust that you will always be enough regardless of what comes as you find the courage to leap from the edge?

Much of the evidence we choose to substantiate our fears is false. The evidence we see is biased because of the beliefs that we have adopted or because of something we perceive when we don't have all the facts. This is where the acronym False Evidence Appearing Real adds clarity. Our lives are not endangered by speaking up among strangers at a party or any of the other hundred things we may dread in life. Yet we frequently fear circumstances like this.

Entering the Gateway of Prosperity requires that we learn to quiet those false signals so we can see proof of our vision starting to manifest right now. We must exchange those beliefs and fears for the belief and anticipation of receiving something new. We must illuminate the dark places with the light of desire for a better life—a better life for us and for those we can serve once we arrive in our personal place of prosperity. We notice our fear, understand its false nature, and step beyond it. We draw courage from the innermost strength we possess and we walk into the unknown with confidence and boldness to stake our claims in the place called Prosperity.

When a feeling of fear (in the guise of doubt, anxiety, worry, apprehension, etc.) takes hold, ask the question, "Where is this fear coming from?". Find the root—the tether that holds you bound—and ask if it is truth or belief. If it is a belief, and it most certainly is, change it with your Permission Process!

Perhaps your obstacles to your Gateway of Prosperity are fear related, but you perceive them as something more tangible. Perhaps you're telling yourself, "I'm not afraid, and I would do it if I could, but there is a real obstacle in my path, physically preventing me."

In truth, aren't all leaps, by their very nature, physical obstacles? Whether real or envisioned, there is a chasm between us and where we want to be. That chasm must be navigated to arrive on the other side—to reach where we want to be.

In real life, chasms can be leaped over if we get enough momentum and lift. And if it is physically impossible to leap over a chasm, then we can build a bridge or fly a helicopter over it. The same is true of the metaphorical chasms we must leap. At first, we may see what's on the other side of the chasm only partially. The full view of what awaits us on the other side will never be completely clear until we actually act, move, LEAP! I didn't know what it was like to have a home in a desert community until I slept a couple of nights there and enjoyed the surrounding beauty for myself—but that was only after I chose my dream to have a desert retreat.

This aspect of believing before experiencing is one of the most difficult parts of each gateway. With each new gateway, faith and the belief that we are enough are required. Seeing it first in our minds, then overcoming fear to leap into the prosperity of the real thing may be difficult, but it is only difficult in our fearful thinking.

When I took all of the necessary steps to prepare myself, I finally just had to allow myself to fully be committed. I trusted the Gateway of Faith and the Gateway of Abundance from my previous lessons. I believed that I would be given exactly what I needed and that I was enough.

Even greater than the exhilaration of flying across that imaginary chasm, I recall the moment I landed on the other side of the chasm. I turned around and looked back to the edge where I had been fearfully rooted moments ago. To my astonishment, I could clearly see thousands of people standing on the other side—people who had been waiting for me to go first. I looked around at all of them and saw their fear replaced with hope.

Suddenly I was filled with an overwhelming desire to reach out and help them leap to where I was. I wanted them to live in prosperity too. I wanted them to come and be part of the community called Prosperity. As soon as I found my footing in Prosperity, I began devising ways to bring them across, to build a bridge for those who would follow.

I believe that people who include "everyone" as possible outlets for their prosperity, experience the highest level of abundance in their own lives and continue to grow beyond the Gateway of Prosperity. Living and serving for something higher than ourselves drives us forward and onward. Relaxing within Prosperity longer than necessary is setting a stage for a new comfort zone. Even prosperity can become a mundane existence.

If you haven't experienced real joy in your life recently, perhaps it's time to reach out and begin extending the range beyond your own personal prosperity. Perhaps it's time to move on to the next gateway.

Your Rite of Passage through the Gateway of Prosperity
How Aligned Are You with Prosperity?

Evaluate yourself on a scale of 1-5 (5 is completely aligned):
1. I experience a feeling of Gratitude for all that has been created so far in my life. I am content that it is perfect and I also see where improvements can be made.
2. I see evidence that I already have, even if in just a small way, everything I could ever want. I already see that it exists, it is just a matter of time before it is within my stewardship.
3. I love myself and others enough to build a solid foundation that extends beyond my own personal needs. As I move beyond survival, I am free to see all the ways I can serve and offer a hand to others. I love the idea of surrounding myself with a community of prosperity.
4. I allow the most courageous and powerful version of me to carry me through my fear. I choose beliefs that help me become prepared to arrive in my place of prosperity and to live there comfortably. I also keep my senses tuned to know when it is time to move on to the next Gateway.

The Seven Gateways

MILEPOST 3- CHOOSING TO BE LED

I look back now and can easily see the problem. I was way too committed to building someone else's dream. But in the moment, I only saw that my commitment was not appreciated.

After being fired, for the first time in my life I resisted finding a new job. I was so brutally beaten that I couldn't bear the thought of getting back out there, just to be beaten down again. I didn't know what I was doing wrong, so I couldn't fix it. My heart wasn't in it anymore.

When I did find a position, it was in shipping as before, mostly working by myself. I took on all the jobs that were distasteful to everyone else. I cleaned the bathrooms, I emptied the trash, I took the abuse of disgruntled customers. An honest job, sure, but well beneath my true potential. I no longer claimed ownership. I no longer threw my heart into my work. I punched a time-clock.

I went to work for the money, not to change the world.

If I wasn't punching the time clock, I was being a dutiful wife and mom. I became compliant. My independent spirit was broken. I had a smile on my face, but my soul was dying. Many times the urge to cry overcame me and I retreated to my bedroom to bury my face in a pillow and allow the sobs to escape. I was baffled by the need to cry. I have a good husband, a nice home, great kids, a job. What more could I want?

As I write this, it is difficult to comprehend how I could have allowed my professional life to become so mundane, devoid of meaning or purpose. I soon found out there was a part of me that was still willing to fight. That part of me would not tolerated the life I had settled for.

I had arrived at work as usual and printed off the orders for the snowmobile parts that would be shipped that day. This particular morning, I was working alone. After pulling the items from the warehouse and boxing them up I experienced a strange pain in my left arm. I continued with my duties in the warehouse until the pain radiated up the left side of my neck and I felt a tightness in the center of my sternum. I went to my boss and told her I wasn't feeling well and that I was going home.

By the time I arrived home, the feeling in my chest had intensified. My husband drove me to the hospital. Minutes seemed like hours and fear crept in as the pain increased. It was my heart. There was something wrong with my heart. I couldn't understand how everyone could be so calm and unhurried as I waited in the Emergency Room. I was frightened and confused. From the look on my husband's face, he was, too. I wanted to scream, "DO YOU NOT SEE THAT I AM HAVING A HEART ATTACK!"

The Seven Gateways

The Seven Gateways

THE FIFTH GATEWAY-
OBEDIENCE

The Counterfeit
In the past, I was obedient to forces that weren't within my truth. As I began to understand the gateways more and more, I realized that in all my jobs I had been obedient to mere mortals. Obedience meant dependence, a loss of control, giving up my gift of choice. I became reliant on another mortal being successful in order for me to be successful. Obedience felt like bondage. I punched a time card and I had to do what my boss said as long as I was on the clock. My mantra became, "Tell me what to do and I will do it. Not because I want to help you be successful, but because I want you to see me doing a good job to prove that I have worth. I am obedient so I can keep my job and not get in trouble. I am a slave to my circumstances."

The Truth
The truth is that obedience is freedom. I can let go of having to do it all, because I can trust my intuition and the inspired shortcuts I receive from God. When I am obedient to the laws of creation, I complete my goals in record time!

My Assessment

The result of living according to the counterfeit of obedience is that rather than throwing my heart into the adventure of something bigger, I close and lock the door on my heart. I am alone and isolated. There is no one I can connect with or confide in. I have to do it all myself in order to protect myself from being disappointed by others.

Taking full ownership and sole responsibility for my own successful outcome is purely arrogant. Pride becomes conceit when I have made the decision that there is no one I can trust. Time and energy shrink in relation to the task because I am the only one who can make decisions, time is used up in distractions that don't even belong to me.

Not only am I giving away my most precious resources (time and energy) to issues that are not my specialty, I am preventing others from doing their specialties, robbing them of joy and abundance. I create imbalance within the universal laws and policies that govern relationships and abundance.

Picture a teeter-totter. There must be equal weight on both sides to maintain a healthy balance. The universe must always restore balance. There is an opposition present in all things within our world for the purpose of everything continuing to flow in harmony with everything else.

Just as there are positive and negative forces that enable me to push off a stationary object (the floor or the side of a swimming pool), there are positive and negative forces pushing against the earth to keep it in its proper orbit and rotation. It is absolutely necessary for there to be opposition - equal pull to equal push. To truly live in harmony with the universal laws of physics, I need to use negative forces to my advantage instead of wishing them away.

The answer to lightening my burden and taking away all the stress is to take responsibility and ownership of only my part. In order to do this I need to do two things:

1. I need to recognize my part. I need to know what my gift is, and only do that. If I insert myself too heavily where I don't belong, or where I don't fit, it is a heavy burden for me to

bear. Indeed, it is such a heavy burden that an equally heavy burden must be placed on the other side to compensate. Conversely, if one side is light as a feather, the other side gets to lighten up as well. Thus, if I work only in my gift (which is the easiest and lightest thing in the world for me to do) the universe must respond by lightening my burden all around me.

2. I need to figure out what I am creating. I need to know the ultimate end result I desire. I may be supporting someone else's creation with my gift, but there must be a specific end result for me, or I am overstepping and inserting myself where I don't belong, as the owner of their creation.

Entering The Gateway of Obedience

All of the gateways up to this point, the Gateway of Faith, the Gateway of Abundance, the Gateway of Charity, and the Gateway of Prosperity flowed to me naturally. I didn't specifically seek them out. They came to me as I went searching for my next steps and my most limiting beliefs every morning.

The Gateway of Obedience was different. We'll talk later about what and whom we should obey. First, I want to talk about how this Gateway of Obedience came to me in a unique way. You will see, as I did, that this gateway is the turning point in arriving aligned.

The first four gateways that we've discussed have been for everyone who seeks for a better life for themselves. From this point forward, we are in new territory. As a reflection of that truth, I had to actively seek, discover and initiate action with each of the remaining gateways through my conscious choice. We all have the choice to build a permanent home in our Prosperity community and create a new comfort zone, or we can choose to continue growing toward ultimate integrity and influence as inspiration guides us.

By the time I reached Prosperity, my morning process had become predictably positive. I was open to learning whatever God or the universe had in mind for me to learn that day. I had never considered this way of learning before. Of course, I had always prayed and read good books to seek out answers. I go to church each week, and I consider myself a spiritual person. But this education was different than anything I had ever experienced. I was developing a personal relationship with God as I asked for answers and received them through an inner knowing. As I followed the inspired shortcuts I was given day after day, I witnessed my life beginning to change in positive ways. I saw that my emotions were both rising in vibration and helping to cradle me in peace. It was in this place that I began to trust my heart.

Up to this point I had felt somewhat alone on my path. I did not perceive others who had supported me until I passed through the Gateway of Charity. Through the eyes of Charity, I saw that others were already playing a role in helping me at the same time I was helping them. When I took that audacious leap into Prosperity and turned around to see all those who were helpless without me, I felt a longing to help them cross the chasm to enjoy prosperity with me. It was then that my journey became a journey of many rather than a journey of one.

Maslow's Hierarchy of Needs pyramid demands that we take care of our own survival first before we can help others. Humans have an innate desire to serve and uplift. If we attempt this too soon, however, we fall down to the base of Maslow's pyramid where our physiological needs and physical survival rob us of the ability to positively influence those we want to serve. I may really want to donate to a worthy cause, but if I can't put food on the table for my own family, the money given can become a burden rather than a source of joy and freedom.

After arriving in Prosperity, I had found a place I could breathe! Without having to worry about the next dollar, the next free moment, the next breath, I began to feel some of that joy and freedom that had only eluded me before.

There was a certain sense of exhilaration with celebrating how far I had come. And there was a definite feeling of satisfaction that I could remain there and be comfortable with my well-earned peace. I was content and grateful in that state of freedom and joy.

It was great to be celebrating, but soon I felt a compelling urge to break a new trail. I knew there was more to discover. My journey was not at its end. My persona had transitioned to that of a leader and guide. I felt more confident in helping others to attain what they desired. I had even been instrumental in helping some find freedom as I had. But I knew there was a level of freedom that I had not tasted, and the desire to lead people to a better place began to fill me. I realized that the path being revealed to me was inspired and for more than just me.

Although the next gateway was uncharted territory, I felt it was mine to explore and create the map for others to follow. This was when I started deliberately seeking change and the next gateway. I began asking for new wisdom in my morning GPS, using questions like, "What do you have for me today?" I felt driven to discover what my next gateway would be as quickly as possible! I kept asking questions and trusting that the answers I received would uncover the next gateway in my journey.

I saw the hints of my next leap several days before it became completely clear. I knew the next lesson I would be learning was obedience, but the full understanding of how that would look and feel wasn't initially made manifest. Here is an entry from my journal on one of those days as I actively sought the next gateway:

> The next quantum leap feels very near. I have been guided to several scriptures about obedience, manifesting intentions on my vision board is a measure of how quickly I obey inspiration I receive. I feel that the next quantum leap is obedience. I have the tools, I am in the right place, I have learned the lessons. I am open to receive. My will is non-existent with regard to the 'how'. My will only comes into play with how quickly I obey.

At this stage, I noticed that in the Gateway of Obedience my motivations seemed more altruistic than before. I pursued the lessons of obedience out of a sense of gratitude and love for those who would come after me. This dispelled the fear that had been present with the first gateway—the Gateway of Faith. Instead of leaping away from a comfort zone that felt wrong; I was leaping towards the unknown and it felt right. It was no longer a choice between good and bad, but a choice between good and better.

Fear took a back seat because I had the wisdom of experience and confidence. I now believed I was up to the challenge. I had more tools in my toolbox and I trusted the skills I had acquired. More than anything, I trusted that whatever I lacked would be revealed to me at precisely the moment I needed it. And the underlying motivation of it all became not who I would be or what I would do after this next gateway—it became more about the people I would bless by obeying the desire for more.

I began to see that the choice to leave a good life in search of a better one is reserved for those who ultimately transition from mortal to legendary. Mortal, of course, is who we all are on a normal, daily basis. Legendary is reserved for those who reach the ultimate distinction of leaving a lasting legacy. These become unforgettable. Essentially, they become immortal and invincible, because their legend lives on long after their physical bodies have ceased to exist among mortals. Of course, this may or may not necessarily imply notoriety, fame and stature. It means they have become unforgettable to those within their reach of influence, those for whom they were instrumental in building bridges and blazing trails.

If you are committed to continuing on beyond your own place of Prosperity, buckle up! I found obedience to be the first gateway where I was tested consistently, even daily. Perhaps a better way to explain would be that I was provided with many opportunities to practice obedience until I successfully made it through the gateway.

Most people get stuck in the Gateway of Prosperity and never experience the freedom the Gateway of Obedience offers because prosperity represents a physical goal. They set up camp or even build a big house because they are basking in the success of achievement. Physical comfort feels good. They ignore or rationalize away those twinges of longing for a new adventure that is bigger than themselves. They procrastinate the desire to reach that pinnacle state where they no longer must focus on themselves where they can contribute and serve simply because they choose to.

They are already successful and are living a good life. It is enough. Their place of prosperity becomes a comfort zone that holds them back from ever experiencing what it feels like to be motivated by love. If, however, we can move when we feel there is something more, even in the midst of success, we never have to be motivated by fear again. The Gateway of Obedience is the portal to self-actualization on Maslow's Hierarchy of Needs. Obedience takes us beyond physical self-fulfillment to a legacy of immeasurable contribution.

If we hold onto the comfort zone too long, we must begin again at square one. We are creatures that require growth, so eventually we will become dissatisfied with what we have, and we will know it is time to move on. If our success has become a comfort zone where we are now afraid of remaining the same, we can always go back to the beginning and take that leap of faith again, followed by abundance, then charity, the arriving in a new place of prosperity. It feels like progress. But unless we can let go of our prosperity in the middle of feeling comfortable, we will never move beyond the Gateway of Prosperity.

As we've discussed before, each gateway is a necessary precedent to the next. The same is very true for moving from the Gateway of Prosperity to the Gateway of Obedience. We absolutely have to feel the gratitude of Prosperity to be open to the sacrifice of Obedience.

I have many times used the analogy of summiting mountain peaks to describe the feeling of finally understanding and embracing the principles within each gateway. At the summit, I have always been able to see beyond the mountain I am standing on to the next mountain. There is always more to learn. As I moved from one gateway to the next, I felt the excitement and thrill of reaching the summit.

With the Gateway of Obedience, it felt that from one day to the next was like reaching the peak of a mountain, only to discover the presence of the next mountain range, even more formidable and enticing than the last. After the Gateway of Prosperity, the Gateway of Obedience was certainly a much higher, seemingly unattainable peak, with smaller summits along the way.

I initially struggled with obedience. It wasn't until I more fully understood it that I learned to embrace it. And then everything changed for me.

What or Whom Should I Obey?

The word 'obedience' can be packed with a lot of emotional baggage. It portends that one is subject to the will of another person. It is submitting in some way to the will of a higher authority, whether that authority is government, a parent, or God. For these reasons, many tend to bristle a little at the concept of obedience. The counterfeit of obedience is that it is limiting. The truth of obedience is that it frees you to stop striving and just relax.

We naturally discipline ourselves to obey directives that we feel are for our good, such as choosing to be disciplined and obey the directive to brush our teeth, because it keeps us healthy.

We all understand that it requires discipline to be successful in life. It takes discipline to get in and out of bed at the right time, to exercise, to eat right, to limit how much television we watch, etc. Discipline helps us obey or live the laws required for whatever results we seek.

Trust and obedience are also quite connected. As we dive into the Gateway of Obedience you will see the part that trust plays as well. The Gateway of Obedience necessitates trusting our ability to receive and interpret the message that comes through intuition when we ask for next steps or shortcuts as I like to call them. Trusting the source of the intuition (whether that is my higher self, the universe, God, a passage read in a book, or a mentor) is also vital in successfully completing this gateway.

When I was approaching the Gateway of Obedience, I realized that obedience required me to build a profound sense of integrity in everything I did—integrity in my word, in my choices, and in my schedule. Part of this includes planning my commitments carefully, so that I only commit to those things that are fulfilling to me, and inspiring to those around me. Some who are traveling the Seven Gateways may already have a level of mastery in this skill of integrity. It was perhaps a skill I was not proficient in and therefore, for me, it seemed more challenging.

As I developed the skill of obedience, my struggle gave way to surrender. With surrender came a physical transformation that is difficult to put into words, but could possibly be described as complete calm. Imagine a scenario where there is much to be done, but being at peace.

The Gateway of Obedience changed my nature. I am not frantic. I have untied the tether that held me back long ago, and I accept the role as a respected leader. I am comfortable in the space of creation where I have all necessary resources, systems, and people who are capable of taking care of all the moving parts. I am calm because I have done this before.

When I first accepted the challenge of the Gateway of Obedience, my first week was a little bizarre, unlike any week of my life before. Although I know that life can sometimes be a storm, for the first time, I was in the eye of the storm. The violent hurricane may have been blowing around me, but I was not aware of it.

Making decisions in this calm state was new to me. After a few days, I realized that the feeling I was experiencing was the lack of fear. Fear no longer motivated my choices.

I suddenly realized how much I had been unconscious of the constancy of fear in my life. Before I had pinpointed the cause of my surreal state of calm, I had not believed it was possible to live without fear. Acting unconsciously, we depend on fear more than any other emotion to help us decide what to do in life. We decide our career because we are afraid we will not have enough money. We decide to get married because we are afraid to be alone. We decide to eat healthy because we are afraid of a heart attack. We are driven by fear. The reason we second-guess so many of our decisions is that our decisions are made from a state of fear. By comparison, imagine making a decision from a state of calm knowing, which had become my new normal, natural state.

Once we learn the lessons of the Gateway of Obedience, we only do what we feel inspired to do, when we need to be doing it. We are habitually in the right place at the right time. Our minds are calm. We see many choices and we can calmly and deliberately take our pick. We stand in firm, resolved integrity and confidently take the necessary steps to receive what we have asked for. We act out of love for ourselves and those we serve, rather than acting out of fear of loss. Living this way is the most fulfilling and quietly reverent place we can imagine.

Until we experience the Gateway of Obedience, Prosperity feels pretty good. Yet, 'good' is transcended by a legendary life that is formed out of obedience. The choice to be obedient to the sacred call means we must leave Prosperity in search of lasting influence, a quest that is so exponentially more amazing, it cannot be described in earthly terms.

Every Result is Dependent Upon Obeying Universal Law

Sharing the principle of obedience to universal law, I am reminded of a client who was very resistant to the idea that he was the one who had to change in order for his goals to manifest. My husband and I sat at lunch with him one day, listening as he whined about the universe being unpredictable.

"If I plant a carrot, I can depend on it sprouting at roughly the time it says on the back of the seed packet. I know about how long it will be before I can eat that carrot. Why can't my goals be that predictable?" he challenged.

I answered him with a question. "Are you as predictable as a carrot?"

If a carrot had the choice to hibernate inside of itself and never allow itself to be cracked open in the cold ground, pushing through the soil until it finally could break free and feel the warmth of the sun, it would never fulfill its potential.

The fact is that we are the only ones who have the choice to change. We are the only pieces of the puzzle that are at choice. That is the Gateway of Obedience. Obedience is choosing to be as predictable as a carrot.

Developing a respect for the irrevocable nature of the laws of the universe is a giant step towards mastering the ability to manifest whatever you choose. Later, you will learn about something I call 'immovable momentum.' Immovable momentum is achieved when you align yourself with the other factors in the equation of creation.

Cause and effect is the essence of obedience. We may not consciously realize it, but we all have personal laws that we pay homage to. There are higher laws that apply to every person on the planet and if we ignore them we will make our lives miserable. The reverent calm that I described in the previous section is a result of living obediently.

The truth is that the universe has physical laws that must be obeyed. For instance, our planet has gravity that pulls us to its surface. If we attempt to ignore the law of gravity, like walking off of our roof or driving off a cliff, we could easily be injured, or killed. Another universal law is that for every action there is an equal and opposite reaction. In the Seven Gateways, this means that if we set something in motion, we can expect change. Yet another helpful law to know and understand is that we reap what we sow. In other words, the things we do today—being kind, being angry, working hard, hardly working—tend to result in what we receive tomorrow. These are commonly accepted laws of the universe that must be obeyed. In fact, it is easy to see and understand how and why these laws cannot be broken.

Of course, we can spend time, energy and resources trying to cheat our way through life, and circumventing laws. Indeed, we see people who are not generous who seem to receive bounteous windfalls from life. For some of these people, accumulating things is the most important value in their lives. This is simply a result of obeying the law of the harvest, the law that says what we sow, we also reap. If we sow a desire and actions that produce financial rewards, we must receive them.

My attitude towards this system of reaping what I sow and towards others who are focused on different values than my own may even affect my own growth. Acquiring rewards or things (reaping) is only one part of the law of the harvest. Giving and serving (sowing) is the other part. If we try to cheat the system, the law will always win. Why? Because it is a law that everyone must obey. Even God obeyed universal laws to keep our planet abundantly producing after He created it.

People who only reap things from life end up with plenty of things, but they also often receive little of love or respect because they are not sending forth what is required to receive that result. They are not obeying the law that says if you are authentically generous, the result is that you experience authentic generosity. On the other hand, those who only sow, never reap the rewards of their service. The harvest withers on the vine and the result is usually sour grapes.

The result of being authentically generous is not necessarily financial wealth. Each law is separate and distinct from other laws. Obeying each law has its own reward. They do not intersect or overlap. Many people look to God for their blessings and think if they are good, they will get all good things. Not so. Each result carries with it a law to be obeyed.

Traveling through the Seven Gateways and experiencing the satisfaction and fulfillment that they produce requires that we adhere to all of the principles involved in every law. We cannot have abundance without gratitude and generosity. There is no shortcut to integrity. There is no workaround to success as a mentor. There is no substitute for service or love. The more precisely we adhere to the laws and principles involved in achieving whatever goal we have set, the more certain we will be of receiving the desired result. This is the essence of the Gateway of Obedience.

Obeying the Laws that Govern Money and Time

In working with my clients and interacting with people in general, I feel that time is elusive for most people. For years, time was my nemesis. I always wished for more time, or for time to stand still for me so I could get more done. Of course that never happened, so I was constantly trying to cram more into my time. But time has laws attached to it. I was trying to cheat the laws by squeezing more out of it than was possible, according to physics. We cannot change the universal laws simply by changing our beliefs about them. We can however, change the beliefs that limit our ability to obey the laws.

Time was a law I had deeply desired to comprehend more fully and obey more completely. I sought to become the master of time, or at least the master of my time. I began exploring its possibilities.

This search to understand and work in tandem with the law of time came at a period of my life when I was chronically late. I would leave my house at the last possible second so I could cram in one more item on my to-do list. I would push the limits of traffic laws, driving through yellow traffic lights, hoping I wouldn't get caught speeding—all in an effort to squeeze every last second out of the limited amount of time that I perceived I had available in my life. I certainly saw no abundance of time. I completely lacked an accurate sense of the passing of time. Sometimes I would think that only two minutes had passed, but when I looked at the clock, I discovered that 20 minutes had gone by.

The very first law I discovered about time was that I am only allotted 24 hours in every day. Although time exists in unlimited quantities and there is never an end to time, I only have a certain amount of time (24 hours) available to me as a mortal woman residing on this planet. Once I had humbly accepted that reality, I chose to embrace it. This resulted in a profound sense of gratitude for having the gift of those 24 hours every day. Rather than selfishly wishing I had more time, I was content and grateful that I was living another day and had important things to accomplish within my 24 hours.

This gratitude taught me to see myself as a steward of the time allotted to me. Each of us is a steward of our time, our money, our bodies, our children, etc. As stewards, we must exercise our use of time with wisdom and loving care. We cannot be careless in how we utilize our time. Nor can we be greedy, acting as if we will get more than our allotted share of time. We must be content with the time we have and know that 24 hours each day is enough to accomplish our tasks and goals. It must be, or we would have received more.

As I pondered more about time, I recognized that the most powerful, beautiful, wealthy, generous, successful people in the world also have only 24 hours in a day—the same as every other human. When it came to time, I had exactly the same resources as a billionaire. I decided to try using my time the same way a billionaire does. I reasoned that by coupling my time with knowledge and skill, just like a billionaire does, I could create and receive anything—even a billion dollars if I am willing to do as a billionaire does.

I studied the laws that govern time and began to comprehend its power and predictability. I learned that time is a resource, just as money is a resource and that the same laws that apply to time apply to money. I reasoned that the laws of time are really the laws of infinite resources. I learned to obey the laws associated with time and in the process time became my friend. Friends support and help each other. I committed to honor the time that I was allotted and treat it as a friend and loyal servant, rather than an enemy with whom I was constantly at war.

I have found that when it comes to immovable laws and principles, I am the one who gets to change to strengthen the relationship.

> *Try this experiment - Listen to how you talk about these infinite resources. Interchange the word 'friend' in place of money or time. See if you would want to hang around friends like you. Or if you are like me, you may discover that you are very judgmental of your money and time and that you take more than you give.*

Since time and money are not dissimilar, practicing more obedience with money was a natural next phase to my newly acquired wisdom. Making friends with money was a natural next phase to my newly acquired wisdom. I wanted to better understand the nature of money and its role and utility in our lives.

When I took my first baby steps on the quest to master the laws of money, I had to admit that I had little understanding of it. I didn't know why money went to some people but not to others. I knew that it didn't come to me as much as I would want it to, so I had to learn how to invite it into my life. It was much like deciding to invite more friends into my life.

The first thing I decided to do was change my relationship with money. If you think that seeking a friendly relationship with money sounds a little strange, think about the more common result of having a bad relationship with money. The principles of money are pretty strict, fail to obey them and money will be scarce. Just as a criminal who will not obey the law of the land is locked away from society, those who do not obey the laws of commanding their resources will become separated from them.

I wanted a good relationship with money, so I sought answers on how to develop a good relationship. Over time my feelings about money became very close to my feelings about time—I felt I had a stewardship over the money that came to me. I love to spend time with my friends, and they love to spend time with me in return. I wanted money to enjoy spending time with me, so I changed my attitude and the words I spoke and even thought about money. And soon we were comfy with each other as we hung out more.

Observe some of the language I changed that created a more positive environment for my resources of money and time to feel welcome. For instance, I now give time to things I feel are important rather than taking time for them. I now give money to my investments rather than making money for my investments. To take something from someone or to make someone do something does not feel friendly or abundant to me. The language we speak and energy we radiate about money and time, invites the universe to respond in a similar way. The universe will bring us positive results with time and money if we speak positively, and it will bring us negative results if our energy towards time and money are likewise negative.

I would guess that most people simply are unaware of the language they are using to speak results into existence. Money, like time and all other things that we seek, have laws attached to them, and the more closely we adhere to those laws, the better will be the results that naturally are a byproduct of our efforts.

This book is not meant to teach you all of the laws on which every desirable result is predicated. We are promised in the Bible (Matthew 7:7) that if we seek we will find what we seek. The highest truths are readily available and waiting for us to discover if we seek them. There is much to learn about commanding resources. I am still discovering the language and energy associated with this subject. My own personal study has included mentoring with three billionaires who surround themselves with multi-billionaires. I am multiplying the effect of one mentor by tapping into their mentors through them. This is called proximity of power. I am consciously putting myself in proximity of a wealth of knowledge about wealth.

We become like the five people we most often surround ourselves with. I choose to have a working knowledge of orchestrating the resources that enable me to serve at the highest level possible. So I have developed relationships with people who can offer wisdom that I can trust. I perpetuate that proximity of power by dedicating a portion of my private and group mentoring courses to helping my clients understand and implement this principle of speaking the language and becoming friends with resources.

My highest mentor is God. He has a lot to say about commanding resources in stories that his servants, the prophets have recorded in the scriptures. You will find, if you choose to work more closely with me that I value true principles that withstand time. The highest truths do not change, because the laws of the universe do not change.

Your Daily GPS Process is the key to gaining the wisdom of the universe, breaking through all limiting beliefs surrounding any subject including money and time. You can receive a video and pdf outline of this process, simply for the asking by going to my website *https://wylenebenson.com/contact* and specifying that you would like the video called "Daily GPS - The One Critical Habit for Success." On my website, I offer several online courses and coaching packages to help you implement the principles you are learning here.

The more closely you adhere to the laws and principles associated with the resources you desire to access, the more efficient and predictable your results will be. Money and time are just two things we desire to have a better relationship with. Every worthwhile endeavor has a law that the result is predicated on. Discover the law, obey it, and the result must manifest.

Some Final Words about Obedience

I hope that you have learned that obedience is very different than grudgingly falling in line or blindly following a principle without knowing why. Obedience is a desire to know, a decision to seek, and a willing exploration of the possibilities of results that obedience to the laws produce. Obedience is proactive and requires trusting in your own intuition. It is actively pursuing understanding and then testing what you have learned. When truth resonates in your heart and you take courage to walk through the Gateway of Obedience, you will begin reaping the rewards of choosing to obey the laws. The result of the law must follow. This is a truth that never changes.

The Gateway of Obedience is choosing to align with the law because you desire to walk the easiest path. The universe has to comply with your desires when you follow the laws that produce that desire.

To make this simple and clear, I have written the formula for reaping the rewards of obedience below. When you desire to become proficient in an area, follow these steps:

1. Ask Deliberate Questions in your Daily GPS practice and seek information from mentors and resources that you trust are knowledgeable.
2. Break through all your Limiting Beliefs about the law and about receiving the result of obeying it.
3. Take Bold Courageous Action Immediately, obeying exactly the inspired action step you received. Trust your answer and step out in faith. Faith-filled action creates evidence that strengthens your resolve to continue being obedient.
4. Gain a Personal Understanding of the Laws by continuing to ask, learn, tweak until you have mastered the law and have made a

habit of obedience to it.

When you follow this formula, the universe must obey and bring to you the result according to the law. The result is always the byproduct of obedience to the law. We do not get the result by focusing on the result. We get the result by focusing on the law. Just as one does not lose weight by being a healthy weight, one loses weight by being obedient to the laws that govern healthy weight.

I would like to end this section on obedience by sharing a very personal and vulnerable time when I was asking for understanding of the laws that produce and maintain wealth. I had learned a lot about what it means to have an abundance mindset, and I had broken through a whole bunch of limiting beliefs around wealth. Still, I saw myself going down the road of borrowing to take care of today's obligations.

I love my dad for what he taught me about hard work and integrity. He regularly commented that he was behind on his work and behind on payments. I could empathize with what he had gone through in his business and personal life. One day I said, "Enough! I want to know what I am missing." Dad was in abundance; he was giving in a way that paid him immediately. He loved his work and he was a master at his craft. So why didn't he have the abundance that is supposed to follow giving in a way that served him?

The answer that came was that he was always being pushed by poverty. Poverty is based in fear – fear of not having enough. Sometimes I felt that he begrudged giving money to his family. It was like taking money from his hard work. I never heard him actually say this, but there may have been an underlying thought of, "It's mine! I worked hard for this!" I know I have felt similarly when I resisted giving money to a credit card company when I know most of it was going toward interest.

My dad passed away over a decade ago and he never reached the point of being fulfilled and complete. He never achieved the level that he could let go of working for money and simply work for the love of his work. What is it all for if you can't enjoy it? My dad was working to survive. He never became self-actualized. Even some of the wealthy people I know are still driven by survival.

Over several days of asking questions with a sincere desire to know what my dad missed (and what I was still missing) here is what I learned: being pushed by love is different than being pushed by poverty. Here's what I mean. When we are selfishly focused on our own survival, we are separate from the world. We cannot reach out and we cannot see the needs of others. Our own needs are too oppressing. When we are selfishly focused on our own growth for the purpose of being our best, we naturally want others to come with us. In this way, we are motivated by love – love for ourselves.

Where the push of poverty creates urgency to survive, the push of significance creates urgency to become the best we can be. There is no fear. We are open to invite others along. Rather than working for the purpose of fulfilling a responsibility or avoiding pain, we can share freely of the fruits of our labor. We have confidence in the flow and that it could never dry up.

Your Rite of Passage through the Gateway of Obedience
How Aligned Are You with Obedience?

Evaluate yourself on a scale of 1-5 (5 is completely aligned):
1. I choose to continue growing beyond my own prosperity. I am willing to proactively ask my higher power to show me my weaknesses so that they may become strengths.
2. I am driven to seek and discover the laws that govern the results I desire. I admit I don't know it all. I am open to learning from mentors, ancient writings that have stood the test of time, and my own private divine revelations.
3. I am motivated by love---love for myself, God and my fellow man. I have stepped beyond fear so I never hesitate to take immediate obedient action on my inspired next steps. I am doing it for me and I invite others to do it for them. I radiate my light and celebrate my growth openly so that others are inspired to find their own source of motivation.
4. I know that with anything I choose to invite into my life, I am the variable in the equation. My results are predictable because I choose to be predictable. I am creating in tandem with the universal truths and laws that produce the results I desire. I focus on obedience to the laws and inspired shortcuts, and the result manifests.

THE SIXTH GATEWAY-
HUMILITY

The Counterfeit
I am nothing. I am worthless. I don't deserve success. I deserve the circumstances I am in and I rely on the pity and generosity of God and others for anything new that I receive.

The Truth
I recognize and express gratitude for the source of everything I am and have. I am teachable because I know if I am still living, I am growing. I notice my human-ness and I embrace my capacity for greatness. I seek every way possible to close the gap in an effort to be in perfect integrity with the best that I am capable of. I do my part and rely on the feedback from trusted mentors and God to continue to improve.

My Assessment

I experience the loss of job after job after job. I compromise my will and determination to be an outstanding performer. I decide it isn't good to stand out because the competition has the power to cut me out of the picture. I punch a time-clock and let others lead. I settle for the scraps that no one else wants to have job security. I accept less, in order to minimize risk.

Entering The Gateway of Humility

Have you ever known someone who achieved great things in their lives and then began to flaunt their success? I have. It is an interesting thing to witness. The power of their message is diminished. It becomes hollow, outshined by ego. When they begin to worship their own knowledge, they lose their ability to be tutored. One of my mentors told me that when I cease to be the student, I cease to be the mentor. Fame can be a razor's edge. On the one side is legendary influence for good, on the other side is a graveyard of disenchanted followers.

We also know people who remained humble in the midst of grand success! For them, fame is not so much a razor's edge, but a straight and narrow path that they choose not to veer from. Remaining pure and true regardless of small or grand victories, depends on one's ability to remain humble.

The Gateway of Humility enables us to create a tangible tie between ourselves, God and everyone else on earth. It qualifies us to tune in to a higher power than ourselves. It cultivates a deeper, almost soul-to-soul connection with those whom we serve. Our personal Gateway of Humility acknowledges our dependence on our own intuition from that higher source, and our dependence on others who play various roles for us: the roles of mentor, student, brother, friend, resource, etc.

Once we walk through the Gateway of Obedience, we essentially are submitting to the laws that govern our world. We begin to recognize our place as a creator within our personal universe. We see the necessity of being a willing student and a mentor to others by sharing what we have learned. We are giving and receiving, teaching and learning, beginning and finishing. We have attained the skill of finding prosperity while continuing the cycle and flow of abundance. When the desire for growth arises within us, we are obedient to the call and orchestrate new and grander ambitions.

The Gateway of Humility follows the Gateway of Obedience for a logical reason. In the Gateway of Obedience, we shorten the gestation time of all our goals and desires and are able to manifest in the most efficient way possible. We learn to tap into powers and abilities beyond our own finite physical and psychological human abilities. However, there is a base human desire that awakens when a superhuman gift is detected within. That desire is to be recognized for the achievement. Perhaps you can begin to see the razor's edge. It is good to achieve; it is good to be recognized for our achievements. It is good recognize ourselves for our achievements. But the weakness of mortals is that they tend to get cocky and think they manifested their achievement with their own power. Nothing could be further from the truth. Without the physical laws of creation, without the people that are drawn to us because of the vibration we are sending out, without the inspiration we receive and follow every day from a higher source of knowledge, we are nothing.

Humility is the realization that most great thoughts and inspiration already exist and originate outside of ourselves. Truth is truth. It was already hanging in the atmosphere when we sat down to meditate. I can give myself credit for taking the time to ask, and I can be grateful that there was something there for me to receive. Since it never was mine to begin with, I am just borrowing the truth, thought or inspiration for a moment to help me create what I desire. That truth, though or inspiration is still out there for others even as we grab it for our own.

Again, abundance dictates that there is always enough and resources are always available, and that includes information, truth and ideas. To continue the flow of abundance, I pay what I have learned forward. I give it freely and easily because I know it was never mine exclusively. Truth already existed in the free creative space.

There are many counterfeits to authentic humility. We will address those a little later in this chapter. However, there may be one big question in your mind. If all knowledge and truth is free and should be freely paid forward, is it okay to be paid the ideas you pass along to others? There are some people who have reached the status of independent wealth, who choose to live an altruistic life, filled with service, giving freely of the knowledge and wealth they have attained.

We live in a world where money is the form of value that is readily given and accepted everywhere for value received. Yes, when you take an idea that you are inspired with and make it your own, you should receive value in return. Being humble does not mean being poor.

To be humble, my goal is to claim my place within the flow of knowledge and inspiration. I also need to recognize the source of the flow. Finding my place within the flow, and realizing I am not the beginning nor am I the end, is the essence of the Gateway of Humility.

Part of being in this constant flow of inspiration is accepting my responsibility and duty to be my best for the next generation. I am laying the groundwork for those who will stand on the shoulders of my accomplishments 50 or 100 years from now.

There are two principles that help us understand this concept of humility better. They are:

1. I see my smallness in the big picture.
2. I acknowledge my vital role in the big picture.

Our Smallness in the Big Picture

Have you ever looked down from an airplane and seen the forests, rivers and highways below and realized just how small humans are in relation to the entire world? In the whole spectrum of the expanse of space, humans are tiny little creatures living on a tiny little planet in an obscure little corner of the universe. I am one of more than 100 billion humans that have lived on this planet. In my own little world, I may have some influence and exercise some power over my life, but in the big picture, I may feel truly small and inconsequential. What's more, everything I have, and everything that I can acquire, is given as a gift from sources that are so much more significant than I may ever become in one lifetime. For instance, I utilize the internet every day. I have no idea if my contributions to the world will even be a speck in comparison to the far-reaching influence this one invention has on mankind.

No matter where we are in life, or how far we've come personally on our journey to self-actualization, we must recognize and accept that we are totally dependent on the gifts and laws of the universe and the contributions of others. The efforts of those who labored before us to create the world in which we currently live are significant to what we currently enjoy. This applies also to those who live within our immediate vicinity in our own community right now. And it applies to all those who will live after us.

As we comprehend our own nothingness in the arc of eternity, the antithesis is also true that we are indispensable to the continuance of humankind.

Today, as I write this chapter, Spacex launched the Falcon Heavy rocket into orbit. I was awestruck by the webinar coverage, the clarity of the photography, the precision of the two rocket boosters returning to earth in perfect synchronization.

I remember clearly in 1969, sitting cross legged on the floor at my grandparents' home in Utah, right in front of the big TV that was more like a piece of furniture than a television. Black and white fuzzy images of the Apollo 11 lunar landing are still etched in my mind. And then Neil Armstrong's infamous statement, heard loud and clear through static: "That's one small step for Man, one giant leap for mankind."

In 1969, the underlying reason for the space race was fear. The untested expanse of space held fear for the astronauts and the engineers who sent them into orbit. There was a different energy with the launch of Falcon Heavy. As I witnessed the Falcon Heavy countdown, ignition, lift-off, and subsequent showman-style ejection of the Tesla with Starman chillin' in his space suit, there was a giddy excitement in the air—on-site at NASA's Kennedy Space Center and across the nation.

Advancement in computer technology and GPS Guidance systems have created precision predictability where 50 years ago, slide rules and teletype machines left holes that had to be filled with educated guesses. Today the energy was that of accomplishment, of confidence. And that could not have been possible, without the pioneering of the early days of the space age. Is there any doubt that we are all connected?

Our Vital Role in the Big Picture

We are all connected. We are connected to something much bigger than ourselves, even bigger than our dreams. When we walk the Gateway of Humility, we make the choice to give up our self-centered lives in favor of a life of service out of love for all of the human race. Remember, that is why we chose to discover the Gateway of Obedience by stepping out of a comfortable place of Prosperity.

Although we are still at choice, obedience literally is choosing to give up our choice. Just as a child trusts a loving parent, we give up control in order to allow ourselves to be led. If the inspired next step is to talk to a stranger, that's what we do. If the inspired next step is to invest in a real estate property, that's what we do. If the inspired next step is to read a book, that's what we do. We become an obedient servant of our inspired next steps. Not because we are slave to a master, bound by a contract, obligation or force. It is because we love ourselves so much that we know by following the inspired instruction to the letter, our lives will be more joyful and fulfilled. If there is a God, and I have plenty of evidence that supports the idea that there is, He is like that loving parent whose only reason for denying the child freedom to play in the street, is to give the child freedom to live another day. And although the child doesn't always understand the instruction, he can obey because he trusts the parent. Or he can rebel in the name of control and independence and possibly find a harder path.

The choice to give up choice in favor of obedience requires complete trust. This is the Gateway of Humility. The choice of maintaining control is steeped in doubt and mistrust in anything or anyone other than ourselves. This is the ego path and it is the path of struggle. We deny ourselves the freedom and clarity of seeing beyond what we already know when we cannot trust the wisdom encapsulated in the experiences of others. Our own logic and past experience is very limited. We are in essence rebelling against our own easiest life.

In choosing to be guided one step at a time, we trade in the pride of doing it all ourselves and attempting to control the outcome, for a legacy of a life created with and for the benefit of others.

There are two parts to humility. Definitely, when we let go of control and ask for step by step instructions, we are seeing our smallness in relation to the big picture. But that is only half of the formula. The other piece, recognizing our role in something bigger than ourselves, is just as key.

We can accept our reliance on, and connection with, all people and the divine. However, we can also clearly see that we exist in the great plan of abundance and even that we are a crucial part in perpetuating it. I am a resource to others, so when I am prompted to do something, especially something that will improve the life of another, I do it—without question or regard to personal cost. This quick action stems from a peaceful knowledge that our inspiration has superior understanding to our limited view and will be beneficial to others and ourselves. In the beginning these actions may need to be motivated by faith, but soon the evidence will show that inspired obedience brings positive results.

There are those who walk through the world saying, "I am nothing. I could never do that. That's beyond me. I'm not good enough." Although there may be some perceived humility in such an outlook, it is not the type of humility that leads to any of the benefits from taking the Gateway of Humility. In fact, this view of humility is more like martyrdom. It is a counterfeit. It will not lead us through the Gateway of Humility, but cuts us off from the benefits found on the other side. The authentic form of Humility is more relative to someone who knows everything is accessible at all times and yet only moves when inspired to. A humble person is wealthy in all aspects of the word, and is at peace with what is currently within their stewardship, knowing at any moment they may feel inspired to shift the wealth.

Romans 8:16-17 declares that we are heirs with Christ. (16 The Spirit itself beareth witness with our spirit, that we are the children of God: 17 And if children, then heirs; heirs of God, and joint-heirs with Christ…). To the extent we are attuned to the divinity within us, is the extent to which we deserve all that the Father has to bequeath to us. My belief is that we don't have to die to receive these blessings. My belief is that we have access to our inheritance now.

Our recognition that we possibly have not yet earned these good things is part of the Gateway of Humility, but is discussed in more detail in the Gateway of Equity in the next chapter. Our acceptance of the gifts we already possess, and asking that we be magnified through our gifts is part of the Gateway of Humility. The lesson is not that we deserve everything because of our own efforts or even just because of our divine birthright. Instead, the lesson is that we are a child of the divine, and by simple virtue of our parentage we are heirs to all our Father has. As we come to trust and allow ourselves to be led as a child, we have claim on whatever is needed in that moment to be obedient and fulfill the instructions of a loving Father who desires to prepare us to eventually receive our full inheritance.

The Gateway of Humility comes in our recognition that everything is a gift, a gift for which we are grateful. As a child of the divine, we have inherited many gifts and characteristics. In accepting these gifts, and magnifying them the best we can, the divine endows us with trust—trust that we will use our gifts and use them to help others discover their gifts. Such a trust brings—and may I say even requires—great humility.

We also have evidence that because we have one gift, there may be other gifts to be asked for and received. As we receive more and more gifts, we raise ourselves from a poverty and survival mindset, thinking and acting as if we are a servant in our Father's house, to a mindset of abundance, believing that we are a son or daughter of a King. The Bible is filled with prophets proclaiming this one principle, that you and I are brothers and sisters, that we descended from the same parents who in the beginning were created by a loving Father in Heaven. One of my favorite passages is from the New Testament:

For as many as are led by the Spirit of God, they are the sons of God. For ye have not received the spirit of bondage again to fear; but ye have received the Spirit of adoption, whereby we cry, Abba, Father. The Spirit itself beareth witness with our spirit, that we are the children of God: And if children, then heirs; heirs of God, and joint-heirs with Christ; if so be that we suffer with him, that we may be also glorified together. Romans 8:14-17

According to these sacred words, we are adopted into the family of God, simply by allowing ourselves to be led by the Spirit of God.

Ultimately, humility is acknowledging that we are great, we are divine by nature! And because we are great, we have the responsibility to use that greatness to further the evolution of humanity. The motivation is not obligation, but love for ourselves. For we know that all humanity is connected in one complete circle. To withhold from one is to withhold from oneself. To bless one is to bless oneself.

Recognizing Humility's Counterfeits

There is an authentic and a counterfeit way to look at all things. Just as a counterfeit $20 bill looks very much like an authentic $20 bill, on closer inspection, it is easy to recognize the truth from the reproduction.

For example, the counterfeits of being introspective could be identified as shy, awkward in social settings, a loner. These are negative and usually inaccurate. Authentic descriptions that usually more perfectly describe the internal reality of someone who is introspective might be intuitive, contemplative, having the gift of discernment. Everything has a counterfeit. Humility is no exception.

One of humility's counterfeits is believing that I am nothing so I can do nothing. Jesus was born in 'humble' circumstances and we never hear of him having great monetary wealth, however, he did amazing things and had profound influence! If you doubt your ability or your worth, go back and re-read the Gateway of Faith, Abundance and Charity.

Sometimes we awaken to the fact that what we have is not enough, and, to some extent, who we are is not enough, because we are not fully living at our potential. There is humility in this perception of noticing the gap between who we are currently and who we are capable of becoming, but for many, it is more like judgment and self-loathing. That is a counterfeit perception.

Some people believe they shouldn't be paid well or that if they are paid well, it means they are not humble. If you have limiting beliefs about this, go back and re-read the Gateways of Abundance and Charity. Do your breakthroughs on your limiting beliefs in this area and you will find that it is not an absolute truth that you must be poor to be humble.

Another counterfeit definition of humility is people pleasing (AKA: doormat, martyr, passive-aggressive). Some people learned early in life that they got praise when they did what someone wanted them to do, or perhaps punished if they were not agreeable. It became a survival technique to do what they were told and either make the person feel guilty or slink inside and silently suffer. To try to figure out what other people want all the time is madness. Most of the time we get it wrong and it backfires. And living this way doesn't make us humble, it diminishes us to non-existence. Each of us is a unique individual with unique opinions and ideas. To be anything else is inauthenticity and the epitome of being out of integrity. People pleasing is the antithesis of arrogance. Both are the furthest from humility that we could be.

Claiming my power while believing that I alone create my own success is counterfeit glory. It will never bring fulfillment and happiness because it is a razor's edge. If I claim that I achieved my success alone, I must also claim my failings. Either way, I am alone. When I invite others into my success as in the Gateway of Charity I am never alone. So authentic humility invites others in. Counterfeit humility excludes others.

The Gateway of Charity knows there are others who are standing at the ready to support our cause, not because we can't do it for ourselves, but because it is part of their passion and purpose to support us with their unique talents and abilities. It is super humbling when I learn of someone who desires to be part of my creation. And it takes authentic humility to allow them in.

Humility is recognizing those who are willing to teach us and knowing that the best and most efficient way to happiness is to invite them in as quickly as possible. Humility is not submission. Although it seems that we must be humble enough to become obedient, it is more a conscious choice to align with the laws of the universe than submit to them.

So if the Gateway of Humility at its purest, is inviting others into our creation, what does that look like?

Surrender to Partnership

The Gateway of Humility is partnership—partnerships with others and with God. It is choosing to give credibility to something outside of our own ego. When we step into the unknown, we are focused on the outcome. It helps to see the outcome to motivate us to move away from a comfortable life, to something more meaningful that takes us outside of ourselves. As you learned in the Gateway of Obedience, we move with total commitment when we receive an inspired thought from outside ourselves. We don't usually say, "I think I will go save the world today." That idea usually comes as a divine prompt.

When we choose to move through the Gateway of Humility, our mission is a partnership with no strings attached. We may have a vision of what the outcome should look like but we are not attached to that vision. We know what we want, but are completely open to how it comes to us. We continuously ask, "What's next," then listen. We work in tandem with our partners, and when it comes, we follow the directive perfectly.

Your Rite of Passage through The Gateway of Humility
How Aligned are You with Humility?

Evaluate yourself on a scale of 1-5 (5 is completely aligned):
1. I am in awe of how small I seem in relation to the big picture, and I also acknowledge my key significance in the grand design of humanity.
2. I have a pure view of my part in my success. I acknowledge my own gifts and dedication. And I feel deep gratitude for the contributions of others past, present and future. I know that my success is a team effort.
3. I accurately understand what it means to be humble. I am neither egotistical, nor am I a martyr. I am a rightful heir to the treasures of the universe. I hold myself to the standard of uprightness that is befitting my royal heritage.
4. I give up control in order to have the most control. I choose the vision and then I am open to how it unfolds.

The Seven Gateways

The Seven Gateways

MILEPOST 4- CHOOSING TO BE WHOLE

In the weeks that followed my release from the hospital, the only thing I had to focus on was my heart. Doctor's orders were simple: "no physical activity and no stress."

So I sat. And I wrote. I wrote to try to understand.

One evening after climbing into bed, I grabbed my journal and started pouring my heart out on paper. When I saw the stark honesty in black and white, I gained a clear understanding of what I had being doing to myself for the first time. The words leapt from the page: "I imagine my half-hearted attempt, when compared to the full commitment I am expecting from God...I have made half-hearted attempts in the past and then had a heart that worked at half capacity."

I had gone from giving my full heart to a half-hearted attempt. My body's response was in perfect integrity with the choices I had made as a result of living a lesser, counterfeit life.

I had received a gift. That gift was a heart attack. The recovery period that followed provided the silent moments that were vital to take inventory of my life and my choices. I had mercifully received the time and space I had needed to find the truth about who I am and how I had been neglecting my gifts. My mind naturally had only been reflecting on past experience and logic to establish truth. I did find truth, but it was my heart that confirmed my discovery. The heart recognizes truth instantly, even if it is a completely new concept. It was perfect that my heart became still, because it was in that stillness that I was finally able to hear.

The Seven Gateways

IMMOVABLE MOMENTUM

Before we move into the final Gateway, we need to understand an important principle. I call this principle Immovable Momentum.

Is it even possible to be immovable and have momentum at the same time? Sounds like an oxymoron, a paradox. The definition of Immovable according to Google is "not able to be moved." Momentum, however, means "the quantity of motion of a moving body, measured as a product of its mass and velocity." In other words the faster it goes the faster it goes. So how can a word that basically means "stationary", be coupled with a word that means "increasing motion?" The terms are almost in direct opposition to one another. Opposition, but not opposite.

Think of two people tugging on a rope to keep it taut. If one drops the opposing line, the rope falls to the ground. If that rope were a bridge spanning a river and someone were trying to cross the river on the rope, opposition becomes very important, even critical, to success! Opposition is two opposing forces pushing or pulling against each other to help us succeed.

Opposition is a force for good. In order for the planets to continue in rotation, there must be an opposing force. For me to stand up from my chair, I must push against the floor, using my muscles to push against the act of sitting still.

Opposition is one of the resources we are given to achieve our desired results. Often we utilize opposition in our physical world to our disadvantage. In so doing we beg to be controlled by outside forces, instead of choosing to release control. An example of using opposition to our disadvantage could be having a definite vision of what we want our end result to look like. We are given opportunities that look a little differently so we choose not to take them.

To be most in control of our physical world, we must let go of control. By sacrificing one's own will in favor of following intuitive guidance while honoring and obeying the laws of the universe, we create the perfect space to embrace the life we have always wanted. This is utilizing opposition to our advantage. This is dancing with the powers of heaven and earth, rather than choosing that we like the Fox Trot best regardless of the music being played. This is immovable momentum.

The last job I had, where I worked for an employer, I was making $12.00 per hour as a shipping manager. I clung so desperately to that job because without it, I envisioned us living desperately poor without any hope of rising above survival level. I was introduced to a real estate opportunity that I was very excited about. I gave this opportunity all my free time and very quickly, I began earning commissions that were double what my shipping job was paying me. Within three months, I could believe that I could quit my job and have more freedom to run my new real estate business. But I had the fear that if my commissions didn't continue as they had, I would have to find another job.

The momentum came when I talked to a business owner whom I respected. I told him about my idea to quit my job and focus on my new career. Then I told him I was concerned that my commissions wouldn't continue as planned. I asked him very solemnly if that happened, would he please give me a job.

The man laughed in my face! He said, "That would be like Michael Jordan mowing lawns for a living." He saw my potential for momentum with this new opportunity. All I saw was the same old dance I had been doing. Once I was able to let go of my old choices, I felt a resolve to make my new business work, no matter what. And that year, I made almost triple what I would have made if I had stayed at that former job. Immovable Momentum was created when I cut off my exits and was not able to be moved from my decision to move forward with the new dance step that was more suited to me at that time.

To help us better understand the concept, let's first look at 'immovable.' Immovable is not immobile. Our most ancient writings tell us that God is immovable—the same yesterday, today and forever. Firm, steadfast, a rock in a wayward stream—these all describe what immovable means.

Science and religion hold to the ideas that physical laws of the universe are immovable. Perhaps immutable or unalterable would be good synonyms. Absolute, ultimate truths are immovable; they apply to everyone, in every situation, all the time. An example of an immovable truth is gravity.

Now let's look at 'momentum.' Momentum implies action and movement, quite the opposite of "immovable." However, when we push against an immovable object, our momentum is increased. Think of swimming in a pool. Can you get more thrust by pushing off from water, or from the side of the pool? There are laws that govern momentum as well, for instance an object in motion tends to stay in motion.

The only variable in the Immovable Momentum equation is me. I have choice. The other parts of the equation—God, ultimate truth, and universal law—have no choice. They must be immovable or they cease to be who and what they are.

Consider the idea that when I cease to be immovable, I cease to be me. I at my best, would choose to align with these inalterable beings and concepts, for the sake of my own best experience. If I choose otherwise, I cease to be me at my best (which I consider to be the real me).

In the same way that God, the universal laws and truths are immovable, I can choose to be immovable. As you will soon learn with the Gateway of Equity, you really do cease to be fully you, when you choose to be anything other than immovable. By choosing to be immovable, you are the same as the universe, God, and truth. You now speak the language of the universe, so manifesting becomes just a matter of time and taking action on inspired next steps. When you are working in tandem with the universe, you are just as predictable and dependable as the sun coming up in the morning. You are in integrity to the highest degree.

When God, the universal Laws, highest Truth, and YOU— are working in tandem, your momentum of change and creation are intensified exponentially. You speak a thing, and it is so. You put something on your vision board, and it is done. You ask for a thing, and it shows up for you. Become predictable. Become immovable. When you do, the momentum at which you create, manifest, and receive abundance can be described only as miraculous.

Immovable Momentum allows us to determine the pace at which our creations are completed. To go faster, or even to experience epic speed in manifesting, we must become immovable. That means we need to adhere very closely to the highest possible truths and make a full invested effort at obeying them. We need to become aligned with governing principles. We must let go of ego and pride, which can include what we think we want or even what we think we need. We adopt an attitude and a lifestyle of humility by letting go of control which in effect gives us the most control over how quickly our life spirals upwards.

To become immovable is pure, conscious obedience—obedience to the laws of creation and obedience to our daily intuitive actions. To gain the most control over the process, we must voluntarily surrender control to the process, and trust the principles that govern them. The more immovable we become, the surer the outcome becomes.

This level of obedience to true principles requires a high level of faith. Even though we have not yet seen the eventual outcome, we believe that obedience to the governing principles will result in the desired outcome. It is nothing less than the laws of the universe that take us where we want to go.

When we choose Immovable Momentum, we could also say that we have moved beyond the point of indecision. We willingly choose to obey the requirements of governing principles because we choose to be in alignment with them. We choose to be the highest and best we can be in all situations because that is who we are. We choose to be immovable to increase the speed and momentum at which all the pieces of our creations come together. At this stage of our development, we cannot be comfortable if we are out of alignment—it goes against our very nature.

The Seven Gateways

THE SEVENTH GATEWAY-EQUITY

The Counterfeit

My experiences are labeled good or bad based on how I label them. I am solely responsible for my choices and I deserve everything I receive. I should be rewarded or punished accordingly. God is just and all powerful. I can only hope to be rewarded if I increase the value of my own personal equity by decreasing my debt with God and increasing my value by doing good.

The Truth

Occasional interruptions are necessary to force us to stop a perpetual downward slide. Water and people tend to seek the path of least resistance. If not shaken up once in a while, the gap between what is and what can be would become too big to span. There is a way to make up the difference between our choices and our intentions. I receive the natural result of my actions; however, God judges the intentions of the heart. He also provides endless forgiveness of debt to those who choose to accept his terms of re-payment.

My Assessment

I have been seeing myself as successful, but only as it relates to another person's success. I expect to celebrate the victory vicariously through the company's success. I naively believe that because I am giving my whole heart, if the creation is successful, I will be rewarded equally for its completion. But it isn't my creation. Therefore, I am not entitled to any portion that belongs to the real owner.

Entering The Gateway of Equity

"Christ says, 'Give me All. I don't want so much of your time and so much of your money and so much of your work: I want You. I have not come to torment your natural self, but to kill it. No half-measures are any good. I don't want to cut off a branch here and a branch there, I want to have the whole tree down. ... Hand over the whole natural self, all the desires which you think innocent as well as the ones you think wicked—the whole outfit. I will give you a new self instead. In fact, I will give you Myself: my own will shall become yours.'" -C.S. Lewis

I now recognize and give equal credibility to my body, spirit and mind in recognizing my creations and my purpose. I am genuinely and intrinsically valuable and important in fulfilling my own purpose. I am the only one who can do it, therefore, I am separate from the success of others and immune from opinions and judgments of others who really are not part of my purpose.

As I began pursuing my own authentic purpose, I began to see myself fully and truthfully for the first time. The Seven Gateways are a very personal journey. Once I claimed ownership of my journey and only supported others as it also took me further along my path, I felt a passion begin to build within me. I now invest my whole heart and soul in navigating The Seven Gateways successfully and arriving at my destination with absolute integrity. Everything is at stake and the whole reward awaits.

Here are the truths that changed my heart in my silent introspection:
1. I have a purpose of my own that deserves my whole-hearted attention.
2. In successfully navigating The Seven Gateways, I can

expect to receive the natural result of giving my whole heart, which is the full portion of my reward.

Equity Makes Up the Difference

"The law of truth was in his mouth, and iniquity was not found in his lips: he walked with me in peace and equity, and did turn many away from iniquity." Malachi 2:6

In a home, equity is the difference between our total debt and how much we have paid towards the debt. It has been said that Christ is full of grace, equity and truth. He is full of equity because he has no debt, he has no iniquity (inequity). He was perfect and created no debt that needed to be repaid. If we look at our own lives, we can possibly get an idea of the magnitude of what our individual debt might be, using Christ's example as an equity measuring device.

He is full of grace, because He extends the same invitation to all, to walk with Him and let Him lighten our burdens. I do my part, giving my all, then I have permission to call upon His grace to make up the difference. He is full of truth because, being perfect and upright, he was in full integrity with the highest truth and immovable laws at all times.

The problem with using this perfect man as our comparison is that we may judge ourselves as so far from perfect, that it is not possible to attain. The beauty of the fact that He was perfect, is that He is full of an infinite amount of equity that never runs out. So He can loan us whatever we need to be in full integrity with repaying the debts we have created, just as He is. And we can arrive aligned at our ultimate destination.

The highest version of our true nature is found within the Gateway of Equity. This Gateway invites us to show the full measure of ourselves to the world. When we choose to step through the Gateway of Equity, we become an open book for all the world to see. What they see on the outside is the same as who we are the inside. Within the Gateway of Equity all our actions, our character, the home and life we have created for ourselves, the way our bodies look, our attitude, the people within our sphere of friendship and acquaintance, are all aligned completely with who we are. We are in full integrity in every area of life and business.

The interesting dichotomy is that when we have not walked the Seven Gateways, our whole day may be absorbed with trying to make people think we are something we wish we were. When we choose this final Gateway of Equity, we simply are. We radiate integrity. We go about our day with no thought to ourselves because we just are.

The way I've defined integrity is more than a value I adopt. It is more than a way of life I choose. Integrity is a state of being that locks into place when everything in my personal universe is as it should be—all the pieces line up. I have and am everything that perfectly fits with the very core of my being. What is on the inside is meshed with what is on the outside. I become impeccable to the judgment of God, myself and others because there is nothing to judge.

Before you reject the idea of being perfect as unattainable, read on.

Alignment and the Mirror of Erised

In J.K. Rowling's first book, *Harry Potter and the Sorcerer's Stone*, the final test or charm protecting the Sorcerer's Stone is the Mirror of Erised. Only those who desired the Sorcerer's Stone for a pure purpose could attain it. According to JK Rowling's fan page "Pottermore," the Mirror of Erised was used as "a superb hiding place, and the final test for the impure of heart."

Before the mirror was moved from one part of the castle to the cavern beneath the trap door in the third floor corridor, Harry stumbled upon it and found that he could see himself with his parents. He felt a new kind of happiness brought about by the experience of interacting with his parents in the present, not just as a memory. It was not real, but Harry experienced it as if it were real.

As Professor Dumbledore invited Harry to try to guess what the Mirror of Erised did, he gave him a clue. "The happiest man on earth, would look into the mirror and see only himself exactly as he is."

Harry concluded, "So then it shows us what we want, whatever we want!"

"Yes, and no," replied Professor Dumbledore. "It shows us nothing more or less than the deepest and most desperate desires of our hearts." Then he told Harry the next day the mirror would be moved and asked him not to go looking for it. He finished his fatherly advice with some profound wisdom when he said, "Remember this Harry, this mirror gives us neither knowledge, nor truth. Men have wasted away in front of it. Even gone mad."

And then finally, "It does not do to dwell on dreams, Harry, and forget to live."

When Harry was living within a dream of what might have been, he was focused on something that could not exist in the present and would only cause him more pain in the end. The happiest man on earth is not only content with what he has and who he is, he knows that it is perfect for him. The deepest and most desperate desires of his heart are already realities in his physical world.

Many get trapped inside this dream world. We either pretend to want what we already have and settle for a mediocre life. Or we set high ideals and shoot for goals that seem to make others happy. Both are usually caused by not really knowing our own deepest desires or what will bring us the most happiness and fulfillment. The reality is that each of us would see something different in the Mirror of Erised.

Must one have wealth, beauty, or a fairy tale romance to be happy? I have met many people who have neither of these, and are extremely happy. So they must not be prerequisite to happiness. However, if I sit looking at that dream, wishing and hoping, it really means that I am not happy in this moment. We are only fooling ourselves as Harry was fooling himself as he looked longingly at his loving but dead parents. The reason is that only when we are content with what we have in our current reality, can we bring what we truly want into physical creation.

Does that seem a little crazy? Maybe. Yet, it is how the universal laws work. Only when I am currently experiencing a loving spousal relationship can I have it in my reality. Only when I open a successful business can I show to the Universe that I can be a good steward of a successful business. Only when I can prove to a banker that I don't need a loan can I secure it.

To seek happiness in something that is out of alignment with who we are destined to become, is madness. To choose what we want and then see how it already exists? That, is to be happy now. Once we can see honestly that it already exists, we open the door for an even more tangible representation of it to manifest. Happiness is not a result of an achievement or acquiring a trinket; it is not achieved by the reaching of a goal. Happiness is a moment by moment look in the Mirror of Erised. Is what I see in the mirror the same thing that I see in my physical world, and am I content that it is perfect in this moment? If the answer is yes, we are well on our way to successfully completing the Gateway of Equity. If no, then it is time to ask what next skill, lesson, or belief needs to be internalized so our world can more perfectly align with who we really are.

So how do we prove to the universe that we can handle what we want? If the universe is a mirror that, like the Mirror of Erised, exposes the impure of heart, then the Gateway of Equity is becoming pure of heart. Becoming pure of heart is the essence of the remainder of this book.

A Mirror to See Your Flaws and Mine

Speaking of mirrors, there is another mirror that holds priceless value for discovering my blind spots when stepping up to the Gateway of Equity. This is the mirror that others are for me. What I see in others is a reflection of what I see in myself. Likewise, what I think about others reflects what I think about myself. For instance, if I look at you and see something that bothers me, I'm unwittingly viewing you in a mirror. I am seeing habits, behaviors, or traits in you that are actually inside of myself. I see something in you that is familiar to me, even if only subconsciously. There is something inside of me that feels uncomfortable. I've been unwilling to address this flaw and here it is staring straight at me! I can't see it in myself, yet I can easily point it out in you.

This reflection is a gift. A gift to help us come back into alignment with the purest form that existed before we acquired the flaw. The uncomfortable feeling is really our true nature trying to tell us we are out of alignment.

We are sons and daughters of deity, and as such, we are heirs to the whole earth. In my belief, as children of deity, we are perfect. We have always been perfect. We came into this world perfect, and by living according to the Seven Gateways, we can return to being perfect every day. Perfect in this sense means in integrity. We can choose every day to be obedient to the inspired shortcuts we are given in our Daily GPS practice, we can level up our beliefs daily to align with the highest truth we are aware of, and we can make choices based on the highest version of us we are capable of embracing in this moment.

I believe that something about the journey to earth from the pre-mortal realm causes forgetfulness. As we enter mortality and experience life as a physical being, we begin to give credit to beliefs that support the idea that our physical world is the most important part of our existence. Without the knowledge of our royal heritage, we create skewed judgments of who we must be. These judgments about ourselves are based on our experiences and surroundings. Our parents and siblings, home situation, social acceptance, religious preference of our families, physical challenges such as birth defects and disease...all of these become the lens through which we see our greatness. A perceived blemish is very uncomfortable to us because deep down we recognize and remember who we are at the soul level---perfect. And we want to be that person again.

Therefore, if I see something in you I don't like, it is an invitation to look within myself and see what is making me squirm. It could be that I see you as being one out of integrity with your word, so the many times I have not kept my word is knocking on the inside of my brain saying, "Hello...do you not remember when you told your husband you would be home at 5:30 and you didn't show up until 6:00?" Even a little out of integrity is out of integrity, especially if it is a pattern. The divinity in me recognizes this and projects the disappointment of incongruity onto the other person, but the truth is always there—I am the one with the integrity problem.

Another way to look at this is in association with limiting beliefs. It could be that you are not the one out of integrity, but have taken on a belief about yourself because of someone's lack of integrity in the past. For example, perhaps my mother forgot she had promised to take me to the park on Saturday and we never actually went. This is not a huge deal. It happens! But, it is not the size of the sin that matters; it is the fact that not keeping your word goes against our most divine and perfect understanding of the integrity that a mother (or father) figure represents. If Mom is supposed to have perfect integrity and she forgot, then I must have done something horrible to not deserve a park adventure. I take on the belief, "I am bad" and attach it to integrity, so whenever I see someone else being out of integrity, the mirror shows me "I am bad."

I know this sounds messed up, but we can trace all our inappropriate judgments of ourselves back to small perceived traumas or big real traumas where erroneous decisions were made about ourselves. We must assume this is the perfect way for us to learn, because this is the way that it happens. If it weren't supposed to be like that, there would be some of us who would continue knowing our divine worth perfectly without ever having to be reminded.

So whether it is something in me that needs to change and I haven't been willing to look at it yet, or if it is a trauma (perceived or real) that caused me to have an inaccurate view of integrity, the person in front of me has now become my greatest teacher. This teacher is pointing out how I can realign myself to the person I have always been. How awesome is that? Rather than getting angry, frustrated, or upset at this person, I should be throwing a welcome party and celebrating that this person is providing the perfect opportunity for me to uncover the decision I made as a child and the misalignment I have been allowing within myself.

The breakthrough process detailed in my special edition book co-authored with Kris Krohn, Limitless - Reclaim Your Power, Unleash Your Potential, Transform Your Life is specifically designed to help you discover and re-align your childhood decisions that are no longer serving you. Go to my website https://wylenebenson.com/

product-category/books/ to find out how you can purchase a copy of this powerful book.

It is often easier and less painful to see imperfections in ourselves in a mirror than it is to ask someone to point them out. So seeing others as a mirror is a gift. When something comes up, we can ask, "Is this me?" If the answer feels like a yes, address it. Changing it is a mere choice away. A choice to be better today than we were yesterday based on the new information we have right now. That is the journey to integrity and a huge step towards the Gateway of Equity.

A mirror gives us an opportunity to look inside, inspect imperfections, and correct them. It may require a little courage for us to ask ourselves why we are bothered by what we are seeing in others but as we commit to the Gateway of Equity, we actually go searching for feedback that we can change, so we can become more of the person we know we truly are. The more fully aligned we become, the easier it is for us to receive feedback with an open mind.

I have learned for myself that anything that bothers me is my stuff—something I need to work on. My alignment is so important to me that I immediately begin an introspection for what may be amiss in myself.

The good news is that as we approach a state of 100 percent integrity, purging ourselves of blemishes and flaws, we begin to love those around us unconditionally. As we become more pure and clear, we see the untarnished spirit inside of them. Remember, they are a mirror. If I am aligned, then I am perfect with where I am right now; so others cannot reflect anything negative back to me—only their true nature. And how beautiful that pure spirit is!

When we are in integrity, it is possible to love everyone on the planet with pure charity. When we understand our worth, we know that every other person who has ever lived has that same worth and potential, and we can love them all the more—even unconditionally—because of it.

Likewise, if someone gives me feedback about something I am doing that bothers them, it could be an opportunity for me to look inside and come into closer alignment. Or it may actually be that

I am posing as a mirror and teacher for them. There may be some truth to what they see, and I will know there is if what they say stings a little. If it rolls right off, it is most likely their stuff they need to work on.

I just had a call today with a potential mentor who exposed a raw emotion by asking a simple question. I could have easily shoved it aside and maybe even gotten mad at her for asking the question. Rather, I texted her back and thanked her! Because of the emotion that was triggered in me, I knew she had hit upon a truth that I had not wanted to look at in the past. That is my favorite thing about mentors, they can share information from a neutral space. It's no great loss to them if I don't receive it, but they are way too conscious to just let a real problem slide.

For most unconscious people, they think they are seeing something in others that they don't like when what they are seeing really exists in them. We tend to recognize around us those things that are familiar to us.

For instance, some people are offended when they see someone whispering and pointing in their direction. Others tend to think they are saying something nice and they feel complimented.

It almost always serves to consider the feedback from others as valid first. Even if there is ill intent. We have so many blind spots, especially in the beginning, that we should still take a quick peek inside to see if we indeed have any issues lurking.

I always can trust my heart to confirm any suspicions. If I honestly find myself impeccable in that area, then I can let it go. If I have a really good relationship with the person who is providing the feedback, I could ask if they have personal experience with that issue. In this way I become a mirror for them and can help them become more aligned with who they truly are.

Acting as a mirror for someone else in this way is a service of love. Many are not in a place to receive feedback, so use your intuition in continuing the discussion or just leaving it. Engaging them in a discussion requires complete neutrality on your part and to proceed without judgment or emotional attachment to how they receive it. When I am in alignment, I can listen impartially. Others can say anything they want to me, without disturbing me or risking our relationship. Neutral doesn't mean emotionally dead, it means you are unconditional with how things turn out and whether the person decides to change or not. It takes a very practiced ear to remain neutral in any circumstance. That is the confidence that the Gateway of Equity brings.

I have told the story often of my mother-in-law who came to visit after a four-hour road trip from her home. She had phoned me just before leaving, so I knew I had four hours to clean my house. My mother-in-law had a fetish for clean and I always felt inferior in that regard.

I spent the entire four hours cleaning while she and her husband were driving. Upon their arrival at my home, I proudly opened the door to my spotless abode, with the exception of one blemish—a drop of ketchup on the butter flap in the fridge. Guess how long it took her to find that drop of ketchup? About ten minutes. And then she offered to clean it for me.

I had, in the past, been prone to go to self-judgment and shame at an offer like that, but this time, I burst out laughing! I had reached the end of my belief that I had to honor the standard of clean that belonged to my mother-in-law. It was enough. I no longer chose her fetish for cleanliness as something I had to copy. I allowed her to have her fetish back, and from that point on I never cleaned up for her arrival. She got to experience me in my authenticity and if she chose to be upset or annoyed, it was all her stuff.

The rest of the story is that for the final ten years of her life, we had a wonderful relationship. She had nothing but good to say of her daughter-in-law, even though my home was never immaculate when she visited. The change happened when I allowed her to have her beliefs and I had mine. I did not receive the feedback as judgment any longer. I merely saw it as someone stating the highest truth for her. She was perfect in her home and I was perfect in mine.

Growing to Perfect Integrity

Impeccable is such a charged word, isn't it? It conveys a feeling of being without blemish, without problems, and is often referred to being without sin. Although we strive for impeccability as we embrace the Gateway of Equity, it takes some time to grow into perfect harmony and integrity with who we are. Remember, we don't perfectly remember who we were before we acquired physical bodies in a world where people are fond of blaming their own flaws on others.

As we test out new ways of being, there are some ways that feel like home and others that feel unfamiliar. Many people refuse to change because they don't want to lose who they are. They think it won't feel good to become someone they are not. They think that doing so would put them out of integrity. In reality, the opposite is true. We rediscover who we are as we align more closely with the person we always have been. Being in perfect alignment, we reach a place that is actually wonderfully comfortable!

Integrity is not a quest for perfection but a quest for aligning with the highest truth for me. My version of perfect is different than your version of perfect. Those differences are okay. More than okay, they are essential! Think back to the Gateway of Charity. If we all have the same gifts, we can't love and serve each other. There are gaps in all of us. If we were all the same, the same gaps would exist in all of us with no one to fill them! However, if we have various versions of perfect depending on our beliefs, values, talents, and abilities then we can serve each other in ways that are helpful. When I need you and you need me, there is more room for connection, gratitude and charity.

If it feels best for me to have a lived-in feel to my home, then I should align myself with that truth. If it feels best for my mother-in-law to have an immaculately clean home, then that is what her version of perfect is. In this way, there really is no way we can compare ourselves to each other. Our version of perfect is based on what we believe about ourselves and the world around us in the present moment. I may choose to change at any given moment. Just as the Gateway of Obedience suggested that I may grow and come to a point where even prosperity is not enough, my version of perfect can change from time to time as well.

I used to have the belief that it was better to have a messy house because I wanted people to feel comfortable. Obviously, that is just a belief because some people are more comfortable in a clean home. I have leveled up that belief as I have found old patterns and decisions that no longer feel good to me. I am growing and changing every day, and so should my beliefs. At the time I held that belief, it was the highest that I could believe. In this way, even a hoarder could be impeccably perfect if he is living according to the highest version he can believe about himself in that moment.

Imperfection and being out of alignment comes only when we know what our highest self would feel most comfortable with and we choose not to change the behavior to line up with it. It would be almost like we are rebelling against our own nature!

When we can say, to our current knowledge, there is nothing inside of us that we have not already addressed or that we are not willing to address, then we can honestly claim to be perfect. When we are perfect—or in alignment— no one can make us angry or diminish our peace. That discomfort comes when the mirror reveals a blind spot about ourselves we have not yet considered, or when we know about it and we are unwilling to change it. When we have that knowledge, we can choose if we want to up-level our beliefs and our behavior to become perfect again, or we can choose to remain out of alignment.

If we are willing to look introspectively when someone points out a flaw, then our worst villains can serve as our greatest teachers. If someone mentions an issue that they believe they see inside of us, we can be grateful for the opportunity to inspect it and cure the defect. We are conscious enough to deal with it when we see their perspective neutrally. We receive it as nothing more than a chance to live at an even higher level.

As we step into alignment, we find that there is never a reason to be upset by something another person says. If what they say is true (I know it's true because it bugs me), then we receive it and repair it, and we can even thank the person for taking the time to help us. If it's not true (I feel completely at peace about it), then we smile and say, "thanks for sharing", then move on. Internally, we can wish them the best in working on their own stuff. It brings tremendous tranquility into our lives when we can take a step back and say "Hmmm, that's interesting!" from a neutral and loving place, regardless of what the person said or did.

Every now and then we may find ourselves feeling a little ruffled at something someone says. If we are open to alignment, and honest enough with ourselves, it will be an "Oh wow!" moment, because we realize we are discovering something we had not looked at before. A life of struggle is the one where we fight or put off investigating, because we don't want to see the truth. The easiest life is one where we immediately shift our attitude and realign ourselves with the new knowledge we just acquired.

As we begin to spot things that are out of alignment with what we choose and who we are at our highest and best, everything becomes either urgent or repulsive. The urgent is embraced readily and quickly. The repulsive is released and turned away from. Excess weight, too much stuff, volunteering or donating in a way that is not beneficial to me and my purpose (yes, even humanitarian and philanthropic efforts can be out of alignment), too little money, a home with a floor plan that doesn't allow space to express oneself, a job that stifles creativity—all are out of alignment and are keeping us from being the perfect versions of ourselves.

Allow me to share a recent experience I had with someone who received some bad news. She shared with a few of us that she was upset because she was just passed over for a job promotion. The others who heard her story said things like, "Oh, you're so sweet I can't believe they didn't choose you" and, "We're here to support you." Yet, they had no idea how to support her.

I asked her to tell me her belief about the situation, and she immediately began telling me about her childhood in a controlling environment and how that affected her current life. She felt that because of her childhood, she would really never excel in her career. I asked if she thought it was productive to allow her beliefs about her childhood to control her life now. She asked what I meant. I told her, "Listen to the language you use. What decisions are you making right now about what you can and can't have?" She immediately recognized that I was approaching her predicament much differently than her other friends had—I helped her see her accountability. She saw that she was blaming her childhood for her lack of success as an adult.

Perhaps it was a little callous to be so direct, but when we are in alignment, there is no need to hide behind false façades. Think of a surgeon who chooses to use the blunt edge of a spoon to do his work, because the sharp edge of the scalpel just seems too harsh. Of course, the opposite is true, and where the spoon would be very painful and leave a horrible scar, the scalpel, although also painful, is sharp and exact, resulting in the least amount of trauma and injury. Precision and willingness to get right to the issue may sting a little. The immediacy may seem rude and even unfeeling. But the experience will be less intrusive overall with much quicker healing.

I may only have one opportunity to impact a person's life for good. I only have that moment, and it is my intention to make a difference in that one moment. My friend recognized that I was not being purposefully or unnecessarily harsh with her, but that I wanted to get the job done as quickly and painlessly as possible.

Be a Third-Party Observer

Another woman had a recent experience at an event where she became upset when a friend yelled her name down the hall of the convention center. She became so upset that she ducked into the nearest ladies' restroom to hide and deal with the emotional trauma she was experiencing. She had assumed the lady was angry with her.

I led her through an exercise and asked her to take a step back from the situation and put a scientist's lab coat on. I invited her to, in her imagination, take out her clipboard and look at the situation dispassionately, as though she were an un-invested third-party observer of the situation. I told her to now review the occurrence in her mind and see it from that new perspective. This exercise helped her see the scene from a completely different perspective; she imagined entirely different intentions on the part of the yeller and was able to step out of upset and emotional trauma.

When we are able to assist people into alignment like this, it opens up a new world of understanding and perspective, helping them approach the Gateway of Equity as well. Their new-found alignment replaces strife with peace and positive perspective.

Mirroring is not the only thing that triggers flaws in our alignment. Stress and deliberately seeking out our next level of growth are also effective ways to see the parts of us that are out of alignment.

I well recall a recent public speaking course that I took in a condensed format (six months of content in a two-week period of time). I was greatly stressed and brought to tears every day as I was repeatedly confronted with my own shortcomings. This type of a situation where there is little time to process through and recover from something that blind-sides you is palatable only with an amazing support system. The course was based in love and I received even more supportive feedback that the suggestions for change, which created a safe environment for growth.

Each day in the course, I was shown aspects of myself I could improve. I had an opportunity to proactively put a mirror in front of me based on the feedback I was receiving. Most days I had adequate emotional intelligence to receive insight into my flaws and defects and chose to change them. Other days, I asked and received the support needed to continue moving forward. It was a very empowering experience.

Sometimes discovery comes through stress, sometimes mirroring, and sometimes from my own inquiry in my private connection with my Maker or someone I trust. My goal in the Gateway of Equity is to find the things that are not allowing me to show myself in full alignment and eliminate them as soon as I become aware of them.

Just as a misalignment in the spine can be more easily corrected when the person seeks professional help early, it is much easier to realign ourselves the moment we recognize our belief system is out of alignment with what we really want. Certainly, the sooner problems are discovered and identified, the less painful they are to overcome. When I take immediate action, I skip the pain of having them exposed at an inconvenient time, when I might lack the resources or immediate opportunity to deal with them appropriately.

I feel that working on myself in private, seeking out those little habits and defects with the intention of becoming more perfectly aligned, is much better than being triggered in public.

Although the daily discovery of blemishes and flaws can be somewhat painful, we are grateful for the discovery process and that we have the tool of giving ourselves permission to proceed. We also have the resource of connection to trusted guides, to help us through to the other side of pain. On the other side of pain is purity and a clearer vision of our infinite worth. As we go through this refining and discovery process, the pain lessens and the shifts happen more quickly. That is when we know we are living daily in the Gateway of Equity.

Aligning with Natural Laws

"For as a man thinketh in his heart, so is he."
Proverbs 23:7

If I am focused on the things that bring me happiness, I am happy. The reverse is true also; if I am focused on results that bring me pain and suffering, even if it is just to worry about them, then that is what I will bring myself.

Having a more intimate relationship with universal laws, I now get it! I create my own happiness and I also create my own pain and suffering by what I focus on.

For instance, as I shared in the Gateway of Obedience, there are certain laws, rules, and universal truths on which certain results are based. An example of this might be movement. We know that it takes less energy to keep an object moving than it requires to get it moving from a dead stop. So if we let a project come to a screeching halt, it is much harder to get going again. If we stay with it, and keep moving it along, it is much easier to reach the finish line than it would be if we walked away and ignored it for a few months or years.

We know movement is the natural state of things. Everything is energy, and energy is in constant motion. Quantum physicists have found that even matter – the building block of (seemingly) solid objects - is energy. That which slows to a stop will cease to exist in its current state, cease to fulfill the measure of its creation, and eventually cease to live!

Look at how atoms are made up of orbiting particles and how solar systems and galaxies are comprised of orbiting bodies. Our universe is constantly in motion, from the smallest sub-particles to the largest super-galactic systems. The universe is teeming with Immovable Momentum, the type of momentum that is perpetuated because of its immovable or immutable nature. The constant and predictable behavior of a thing is what gives it purpose, shape, constituent elements, and life. To the extent that we are willing to align ourselves with that predictable movement, discovering and obeying the ebb and flow of the natural laws of motion and accumulation, we will find the universe offers its assistance in accomplishing our desires much more efficiently than if we tried to fight the laws of nature and set our own pace.

The more closely we align with the natural momentum of the universe, and the more parallel we are to its natural rhythm, the more immovable we become as well. Immovable Momentum is keeping things moving in the direction of focus while staying obedient to the laws that will get us where we want to go in the shortest gestation period.

Thus, it is my desire to remain in integrity with Immovable Momentum. This keeps me in flow with the energy of the universe as I am simultaneously remaining in integrity with my own truth. One way I stay in Immovable Momentum is to check in with my goals daily so they never slow to a stop. This puts me in a very desirable position. Just as surely as an action produces an equal and opposite reaction, my momentum will most definitely result in the desired outcome—as long as it is in alignment with the natural laws that surround it. A rocket ship has to align with the orbit of a celestial body before it can leap into orbit. We must align with the energy and laws that govern a new goal we are stretching to reach before we will be allowed into its atmosphere.

In the Gateway of Obedience, I offered a suggestion that if we become as obedient as a carrot, our gestation time can be just as predictable as a carrot. Yet, on the back of the seed packet, the time from seed to table can vary from one to three weeks. Why the large gap in gestation? What makes the difference between one and three weeks? It's not the carrot; it's the circumstances it lives in. The carrot is affected by how much sun it receives, how much water, how cold or hot the temperature is, how deep it is planted, etc.

If I want to become a carrot farmer, I first need to learn all the natural laws surrounding growing carrots. I prepare the soil, plant a carrot seed, and provide it with water and nutrients on the schedule and in the quantities that are optimum. I ensure I plant in a place where the seed will have sufficient water, warmth, and other things it needs. The more closely I follow the proven directions given by the universe for growing carrots successfully, my chances of harvesting carrots in the shortest gestation period is increased.

Conversely, I could believe that I am an especially gifted farmer and an heir to greatness. I could believe that my position as this regal farmer exempts me from aligning myself with the governing laws of successfully harvesting carrots. I could take some carrot seeds out of the package and throw them at the hard ground. I could ignore them—never water them, or weed them. If I really believe with all my heart and focus on the belief that I am a gifted farmer and I will get beautiful sweet carrots regardless of how I plant and care for my carrots, what can I expect from that effort? Not a single carrot. If I have strong belief, but my actions are out of alignment with what I know to be the highest truth, then I am not immovable as the laws are immovable. And I will not have Immovable Momentum.

But let's say I do some of the necessary steps, like prepare the soil and plant the carrot seeds. I ensure they get sunshine, etc. The one thing I don't do is see to it that they get enough water and nutrients. Sure, there are some nutrients already in the soil, and a little rain falls during the growing season, so I will likely harvest some carrots. However, they may not be as plump, sweet, or nutritious as they would be had I better aligned myself with the known laws of growing carrots. If the farmer, does not give the carrot enough water, that one variable will lengthen the gestation or diminish the return that can be expected because a lack of water does not align with the needs of the carrot.

When I, as the farmer, become immovable to the laws that govern carrot growing, and perfectly obey them, the gestation period is predictable. It is predictably the shortest possible with the greatest reward. How closely I align with known laws is the immovable part.

The momentum part of Immovable Momentum refers to how fast I get my results. Gestation becomes a predictable, known quantity when we align ourselves with natural laws. By predictable, I mean that we are able to predict timeframes to the extent we understand the laws. Success comes within the fastest possible time frame according to our alignment with universal law.

We receive the results of whatever laws or beliefs we align ourselves with. This is true of positive results and negative results. We reap what we sow. There is a result for each action we take. If we align ourselves with laws of doing good to others, we will reap the associated positive results. If, however, we align ourselves with laws of selfishness, crime, abuse, addiction, etc., we will reap those negative results. If we continue to align ourselves, unchecked, with these negative laws, we may eventually experience disaster.

The Highest Truth

Immovable Momentum comes when aligning ourselves with the highest truth. By highest truth I mean the truth that is closest to the laws that God and the universe obey. Since I am personally on a constant quest of uncovering truth in an even higher degree, I may not know exactly what the absolute highest truth is right now. Does that mean I have to keep searching before I obey? No, for it is in the very act of implementing and obeying what I have previously learned that takes me to the next level of knowledge.

As I am constantly seeking to be in alignment, and daily seeking to be as close to the highest truth possible, I will be in a very good place to receive more when I am ready for it. The Gateway of Humility taught me to ever be the student seeking my next lesson. Every seed of truth that is planted and nurtured grows to more truth.

I encourage all my clients to be entirely open to tiny tweaks and corrections. I help them focus on the daily task of actively seeking the highest truth with which they can align themselves at their current phase of development. This discovery of truth often comes in steps. For example, I may write a question or write a statement of truth the way I currently understand it, and put it on my vision board. I check in with it daily and listen for any new thoughts that add to what I already perceive as truth. After a couple of days or even weeks of looking at the words that seemed perfect in the moment I wrote them, I suddenly find that a keyword will jump out at me and grab my attention because it now feels out of alignment. Based on what I have learned since writing it, there is something that feels off. It is not close enough to the truth I now believe. In those moments I realize that the truth I am just now seeing was there the whole time. I didn't see it in the beginning because I wasn't the person I needed to be in order to see that truth. It wasn't that I was ignorant or not paying attention when I first wrote my vision. What I wrote was absolutely in alignment with what I knew in the moment I wrote it. What changed?

Did the truth change? No, the truth is immovable, remember? Did the angle of the light on my vision board change? Possibly. Most likely though, it was me. I changed! That is, I grew to accommodate my own higher truth. There was something within me that finally developed to the point where I could see it differently. That is what allowed the corresponding shift in my perspective.

In altering the words on my vision board, the whole picture changes. So then, I get to sit with the words I have written, get comfortable with them and see if I am willing to accept the new word or phrase that more closely aligns with the immovable nature of a higher truth. Of course, I also have another choice in this situation (one which I am not willing to entertain) and that other choice is to stubbornly or absent-mindedly keep the statement the way it is, forever freezing my progression at that level.

Many people go to great lengths to create elaborate visuals and recordings of their affirmations and goals. I do have a system of recording and reading my declarations daily. I value this process, but

I don't plan to keep it static for any length of time. My knowledge changes moment to moment, and I am open to leveling up to the highest truth on that same timetable. My vision board always has words crossed out and new words written in that support my creation better and put me even more in an immovable space of momentum.

Isn't it interesting that being open to change takes us to being even closer to becoming unchangeable?

"In matters of style, swim with the current; in matters of principle, stand like a rock."

Thomas Jefferson

With all of this movement, how do we ensure that we are moving in the correct direction? In the same way that a kite moves in the natural direction of the wind, we find that stabilizing it with a tail helps the kite make those tiny course corrections of new wind patterns, without overcorrecting and causing it to drop out of the sky. As we employ all of the gateways we've learned, our personal rudders (proactively aligning with our highest truth in our Daily GPS) will keep us on the correct course.

Our personal rudder, like the tail of a kite, is our internal desire for a free soul. In the Gateway of Charity and the Gateway of Humility, we find that we rely on the gifts and support of others to find our way and achieve our potential. We develop partnerships that are synergistic in producing exponential results as we spur one another on to greater heights. The realization that 'it's not all about me' has a tremendous influence on our rudder, keeping it straight and true, and giving us small course corrections by receiving feedback from others, as we encounter forces that would deter us from our true course. Mentors and other guides can read the wind by watching the tail of our kites, perhaps better than we can in our first attempts at climbing to new heights.

One of my mentors regularly shares his formula for achieving success as identifying and breaking through one thousand limiting beliefs. Is his formula absolutely true? Maybe, maybe not. Do you want it to be true? Is it sound advice? Only you can know...and you will only really know for sure when you try it! Track the number of limiting beliefs that comes up as you move through the space of Creation towards the life you are committed to building for yourself.

Each time you feel a low vibration emotion such as resentment, anxiety, doubt, anger, frustration, take a moment and ask, "Where is this coming from?" Your intuition will show you and give you the words. Then either choose into a new belief or actually go back to the origin of the limiting belief, when a destructive decision was made at an emotionally charged moment. (Refer to my special edition of the book *Limitless - Reclaim Your Power, Unleash Your Potential, Transform Your Life* for the entire origin breakthrough process.)

As you commit to and work through one thousand limiting beliefs, your life will be transformed. Happiness awaits those who can step out of fear and pain and step into love and faith simply because they choose to. Does it take one thousand breakthroughs to create a successful life? I don't know. Does it take more than ten? Probably. I still notice limiting beliefs coming up and I passed my tenth breakthrough a long time ago, but they are less frequent and more easily dismissed than ever before.

My suggestion is to choose to give yourself permission to proceed through all your limiting beliefs. Visualize your daily success in detail and notice when any fear emotion surfaces. Make the commitment to take action immediately as those emotions arise by leaving behind the underlying belief and keeping on your path to success.

When we know who we are and what we are creating, we can stay in Immovable Momentum regardless of the resistance that comes up. When the reason we are moving is bigger than the limitation, we find ourselves more easily able to hold firm to what we know to be true.

Align yourself with a cause that lights a fire inside your soul. Follow the course that stokes the fire.

Final Advice

A final piece of advice that someone once gave me: "If you will do for two years what others will not, you will have for the rest of your life what others only dream about."

How do we apply this sound piece of advice? One way is to

practice the Daily GPS I have taught you. Take a moment to connect with your goals and your highest source of inspiration. Obey immediately, the inspired shortcuts you receive through inspired guidance. Then proactively seek the reasons behind any negative limitations that are holding you back.

Have the courage to live your life in the space where all creation happens. You will feel like you are in a freefall with no solid ground to stand on. Yet, in time, you will grow to love this feeling and you will never want to live without it. Remember, in the creative space, we can't see the next steps or the outcome, but there is a Power outside of us who can. What you can depend on is the accuracy of the information you receive. I have never received an inspired hint that didn't eventually play out as the best and most efficient path. You have this one tool, your Daily GPS, to guide you every step of the way. If you can trust that one shortcut at a time is enough, you can have anything you choose.

The Gateway of Abundance is waiting for you at the very moment you walk through the Gateway of Faith. Abundance exists, faith launches you into the middle of it. The Gateway of Charity gives you all you lack through gifted team members and accepting your own greatness. As you give your whole self to excellence, you open the floodgates of wealth and influence. Next, feel gratitude for what has already been created, because this is your ticket to the Gateway of Prosperity. It's great to celebrate and yes, it's good to bask in your success and the blessing of results well earned. But when you feel the pull of a higher mission and purpose, risk it all by moving forward again out of sheer obedience and love for yourself and anticipation of what's next! If you stay put, your place of prosperity becomes a comfort zone that will eventually feel more like a prison.

After the Gateway of Obedience, which propels you back into your creative space, resist the urge to stroke your ego of how easy life is with the discipline you have fostered in your life and career. Remember who you were before you walked this path and remember the support you receive through the Gateway of Charity from all people past, present and future who have inspired you to become who you are today. And above all, remember your source of inspiration, the One who illuminates the shortcuts for you. The Gateway of Humility will allow you to continue receiving the abundance and wealth you have enjoyed so far, and open the way for even more to be experienced!

And finally, the Gateway of Equity allows us to feel the peace of alignment that comes when the spirit is allowed to speak, and even lead. The Gateway of Equity is defined by living in integrity every day with the highest truths we can embrace in the moment, and then calling upon and accepting the helping hand of Jesus Christ to close the gap. He has the limitless ability to help us see beyond the physical to a higher commitment of Immovable Momentum, integrating body and spirit, aligned with the same truths that God subscribes to. Christ's sacrifice is sufficient for us to choose every day to change and become more aligned with universal laws, being the student to constantly level up our knowledge of them.

When Jesus is walking with me and I accept Him as my teacher, it's a gentle invitation to receive instruction. If I choose to force my will, it takes longer. My way is always striving but never arriving. God's way is arriving in record time because the way is simple and easy. Jesus has been called the Good Shepherd. He rescues the lost and directionless sheep by calling them to Him. There is no force, only an outstretched hand.

Striving	**Arriving**
Fight or Flight	Faith
Survival	Gratitude
Forcing	Allowing
Fear	Love

The path to peace and freedom in wealth, wisdom, strength, honor and the power of positive influence lies in your dec-ision to enter through the Seven Gateways. When you do, you will courageously take both baby steps and quantum leaps. You will integrate what you learn into your very being every day. In this way you and I can be perfect every day.

Some look at perfection as an unattainable goal. The fact is that each of us is capable of being in perfect integrity every day. The problem with most people is that they try to jump forward to perfection without walking through the Seven Gateways first. It is possible to arrive aligned. Give yourself permission to try.

There are many lessons beyond what we learn in the Seven Gateways. Each of us is on our own path with experiences unique to us. However, these seven principles along with the daily practice of gratitude, courageously choosing to let go of limiting beliefs in order to align with truth, and connecting with God are, together, the foundation that supports us through every new level toward perfection.

Jesus Christ is the equity we need to be complete, whole and perfect. He has promised us that if we give ourselves to Him that He is able to carry us. In fact, the deed has already been done. He has already sacrificed His life for our benefit. He did the suffering, so we don't have to. All we need to do is turn to Him, ask and receive the amount we lack to make up the difference so we can be whole just as He is whole, and become joint heirs with Him in our Father's eyes. Even before walking through the gateways, you were eligible. However, with the Seven Gateways you have been prepared on the conditions He has established, that you become perfectly aligned with Him and the Father. You are worthy to receive His mercy. As He gives, He is filled. His pure love is infinitely abundant and cannot be diminished.

Your Rite of Passage through the Gateway of Equity
How Aligned Are You with Equity?

Evaluate yourself on a scale of 1-5 (5 is completely aligned):
1. I see myself as I am reflected in the eyes of others. I am grateful for my teachers who are as a mirror, showing me the greatness and the weakness within me. I eagerly make changes to find the best that lies within me. I am also willing to be the mirror for others. I am able to step outside of the situation as a third party observer. I know that what others see in me is only a recognition of what exists within them.

2. I acknowledge that each of us is on our own path and at a different level of understanding of the highest truth. As such, each of us has our own version of perfect at any given moment in time. Every person's journey to integrity, alignment and perfection is as personal and unique as each individual.
3. I am committed to daily seeking the highest truth and aligning to the best of my ability with that truth. I accept the guidance and support offered to me by divine and earthly mentors. I let my Spirit lead, trusting that I am able to discern truth.
4. I give my best every day and seek the infinite equity of Jesus Christ to make up the difference. "Be ye therefore perfect, even as your Father which is in heaven is perfect." -Matthew 5:48.

The Seven Gateways

EPILOGUE

My wake-up call was a heart attack. The heart recognizes truth. The heart is the place where earthly purpose and divine connection come together. For me, a heart attack was not a bad experience, it was a blessing and a gift. It is perfect that my heart became the focus of my every waking moment so I could discover the way I best contribute to the world. Without the heart attack I would never know that I have a gift for connecting with people through their heart's purpose. The heart is also the receptacle for inspired truths, which is what The Seven Gateways is based on.

I celebrate you for making the choice to pick up this book and follow the map to integrity in all areas of your life, hopefully before you are forced to make a change because of a life-altering experience.

You are not finished. You have passed through The Seven Gateways but you are not done. Your next level awaits. You will soon feel the pull of your next challenge. The difference this time is that you have walked the path and you are familiar with the map. Don't procrastinate until fear forces you outside your comfort zone. This time, take a leap of faith with full knowledge that abundance is on the other side of the Gateway of Faith.

You know the way, go through the gateways again step by step with your final destination clearly outlined. You will only add to the wisdom you gained on your first journey. You may even find that you can now lead others in ways you never dreamed possible.

This is just the beginning. You now have the map that shows you the way to grow beyond your previous limitations. You already have permission to be who you were created to be in the highest degree! Now you can truly embrace your calling, fully express yourself and begin impacting the world with your unique contribution, standing tall and confident before God and your fellow man. With The Seven Gateways, you can rise above your fears and become more than is reasonable on your own. You have permission to be here. You are expected to grow beyond the talents you have been granted. You are capable of becoming a person of integrity, perfected in Christ.

This book is not finished, but it is enough. I am daily inviting divine tutoring, discovering more blind spots, understanding deeper the hidden treasures within the ancient scriptures, receiving inspired next steps that prepare me for what is next. I am not finished, but I am enough.

I encourage you to make a daily ritual of connecting with God through your own Daily GPS, courageously asking for shortcuts, boldly acting on the inspired messages you receive and then basking in your prosperity. Once you arrive in your own place of prosperity, I invite you to step beyond it by giving your whole heart to loving yourself and others as you create your perfect life of fulfillment and happiness.

THE END

*"And whatsoever ye shall ask the Father
in my name, which is right,
believing that ye shall receive,
behold it shall be given unto you."
3 Nephi 18:20, The Book of Mormon*

ENDNOTES

Covey, Stephen. "Habit 6: Synergize." https://www.franklincovey.com/the-7-habits/habit-6.html.

Frankl, Viktor E. *Man's Search for Meaning*. Biddeford, ME: Beacon Press, 2006.

Heritage Foundation, The. "The War on Poverty After Fifty Years." 2014. https://www.heritage.org/poverty-and-inequality/report/the-war-poverty-after-50-years.

Jobs, Steve. "On Product Design." 2011.

Krohn, Kris and Benson, Wylene. *Limitless - Reclaim Your Power, Unleash Your Potential, Transform Your Life*. CreateSpace, 2017.

Maslow, Abraham. A Theory of Human Motivation. New York: Start Publishing, LLC, 2013.

Mormon, The Book of. http://bookofmormon.online/home.

Rowling, J.K. "The Mirror of Erised." https://www.pottermore.com/writing-by-jk-rowling/the-mirror-of-erised.

Rowling, J.K. *Harry Potter and the Sorcerer's Stone*. UK: Pottermore Publishing, 2015.

Spacex. "The World's Most Powerful Rocket." https://www.spacex.com/falcon-heavy.

Williamson, Marianne. *A Return to Love: Reflections on the Principles of "A Course in Miracles."* New York: HarperOne, 1996.

Ziglar, Zig. "Make a Choice to Take a Chance or Your Life Will Never Change." 2018.

www.ingramcontent.com/pod-product-compliance
Lightning Source LLC
Chambersburg PA
CBHW070059020526
44112CB00034B/1750